WO

06 MAR 07

05. S

D0546126

HAPP 09. 01. 08

'Schoch proves himself a genial guide ... a sound introduction to important strands of religious and philosophical thought.'
Alain de Botton, *Daily Telegraph*

'An intellectual exploration of the best kind, a rigorous dusting ...n of ideas compelling us to think harder and better about what ...'s most precious prize.' Melanie McGrath, *Sunday Telegraph*

'A quietly revolutionary new book' *Irish Examiner*

'Indispensable ... witty and stimulating'
Hugh MacDonald, *Glasgow Herald*

...sting anecdotes ... [the book] offers lots of leads to ... interested in learning more.' Ivo Mosley, *Daily Mail*

... and original' Charlotte Northedge, *Psychologies*

...rational in offering the reader ways to think about ...ess ... Schoch's analysis will hit home for many ...' Helen Boylan, *Sunday Business Post*

amusing

700030024289

... is Pro... ...he History of Culture at
... of London, where he is also Director of the
...anities and Social Sciences. His previous
...eare, Queen Victoria and burlesque.

The Secrets of
HAPPINESS

*Three thousand years of
searching for the good life*

RICHARD SCHOCH

PROFILE BOOKS

By *the same author*
Not Shakespeare
Queen Victoria and the Theatre of her Age
Shakespeare's Victorian Stage
(ed.) Victorian Theatrical Burlesques

WORCESTERSHIRE COUNTY COUNCIL	
428	
Bertrams	20.01.07
152.42	£8.99
WO	

To my mother

This paperback edition published in 2007

First published in Great Britain in 2006 by
Profile Books Ltd
3A Exmouth House
Pine Street
London ECIR OJH
www.profilebooks.com

Copyright © Richard Schoch, 2006, 2007

1 3 5 7 9 10 8 6 4 2

Typeset in Poliphilus by MacGuru Ltd
info@macguru.org.uk

Printed and bound in Great Britain by
Bookmarque Ltd, Croydon, Surrey

The moral right of the author has been asserted.
All rights reserved. Without limiting the rights under copyright reserved
above, no part of this publication may be reproduced, stored or introduced
into a retrieval system, or transmitted, in any form or by any means (electronic,
mechanical, photocopying, recording or otherwise), without the prior written
permission of both the copyright owner and the publisher of this book.

A CIP catalogue record for this book is available
from the British Library.

ISBN-10 1 86197 989 4
ISBN-13 978 1 86197 989 6

Contents

Introduction

Unhappy is the story of happiness. More than two thousand years ago, when the ancient Greeks first thought about what constitutes 'the good life', happiness was a civic virtue that demanded a lifetime's cultivation. Now, it's everybody's birthright: swallow a pill, get happy; do yoga, find your bliss; hire a life coach, regain your self-esteem. We have lost contact with the old and rich traditions of happiness, and we have lost the ability to understand their essentially moral nature. Deaf to the wisdom of the ages, we deny ourselves the chance of finding a happiness that is meaningful. We've settled, nowadays, for a much weaker, much thinner, happiness: mere enjoyment of pleasure, mere avoidance of pain and suffering. Somewhere between Plato and Prozac, happiness stopped being a lofty achievement and became an entitlement.

We can reject this modern enfeeblement of happiness. We can recover its ancient traditions, the traditions that began in the West with the philosophers of Athens and in the East with the anonymous Hindu sages of the Axial Age. We can, with no exaggeration, call these traditions a secret, so unpractised, if not entirely obscured, have they become. Yet the secret will not resist our attempt to find it.

∾

Over the past decade, behavioural scientists, neuroscientists and psychologists (including a Nobel laureate from Princeton) have been working to measure reported levels of happiness and to identify its causes. Their methods are droll. In one 'experience sampling', participants carry internet-ready palmtop computers twenty-four hours a day. When an alarm sounds on their palmtops, the participants – who have been trained to respond with Pavlovian mechanicity to aural stimulation – stop what they're doing and complete an on-line survey about how they feel about what they've just stopped doing. Back in the laboratory of happiness, technicians download this data and then plot a graph showing each participant's happiness peaks and troughs over time. In case the guinea pigs have tried to outfox their masters – pretending to be happier or unhappier than they actually are – brain scans are used to confirm their testimony. (The participants, it can be revealed, are honest.)

What do the surveys say? Sex, no surprise, makes everyone feel better. The second best thing is having a drink after work with your friends. Work itself – challenging, rewarding and secure employment – also contributes greatly to happiness. Commuting, however, makes us miserable. Well, almost all of us. Four per cent of respondents claimed to *enjoy* traffic jams. (Who could these people be?) If you believe the statistics, it's pretty easy to make yourself happy: live within walking distance of an enjoyable and secure job, prop up the bar with your friends, and then go home and have sex. Happiness, the secret revealed!

Enter the economists. Suddenly, they care about how you feel. Which is odd because generally they care about what you buy. Actually, the real oddity is that economists *do* regard happiness as something you can buy. As some of them now propose, we should stop looking for happiness in material prosperity and start looking for it in whatever gives us satisfaction, whether rewarding work, a supportive family or a vibrant community. At a time when financial prosperity is assured for many, though by no means all, in the industrialised world, happiness has become the ultimate luxury item.

Happiness is also a growth industry. Self-help books generate $1 billion in annual sales, while the global market for anti-depressants

(O true apothecary!) stands valued at an astounding $17 billion. The 'desire industry' – whose titans are Botox jabbers, personal trainers and lifestyle gurus – rakes in even more. (So reports the earnestly named Work Foundation.) As the snake-oil salesman with a Harvard MBA would say, it's one vast marketing opportunity. Yet it hardly matters which product you choose, the economists tell us, because what you value is not the product but what it can do for you. You drink the elixir of happiness not because you like elixirs but because you like happiness.

The happiness economists are part of the new breed of neo-Benthamites. Now some explanation for those of us who are not experts in microeconomics. Jeremy Bentham, the eighteenth-century English legal philosopher, believed that every person strives to become happy by maximising pleasure and minimising pain. (He, in turn, had relied upon a distorted view of Epicureanism, the ancient Greek philosophy of living for pleasure, of which more anon.) Bentham wanted the government to enact laws that would give people the freedom to pursue happiness in whatever way they judged best.

Today's neo-Benthamites believe that governments should implement an interventionist 'happiness-based approach to public policy'. Supportively, they want politicians to stop worrying about our income and start worrying about our emotions. They lobby for legislation to foster not wealth and prosperity but feelings of satisfaction and contentment. Surprisingly, the political secrets of happiness include higher marginal tax rates (to stop us from working so hard), restrictions on labour mobility (to keep families together) and redistribution of wealth (to makes us less anxious about income disparity). But what next? A Department of Happiness?

Quitting the laboratory and the library, I found myself both amused and dejected. On the one hand, I had fun learning about the latest trends in 'hedonic psychology' and a 'happiness-based approach to public policy'. On the other hand, I found that none of this helped me to find the secret of happiness. Not that the results of the research were unclear. What could be more lucid than the expres-sion of happiness brainwaves along the graphed co-ordinates of 'x' (intensity) and 'y' (time)? No, the flaw was introduced much earlier in the process: not in the answers generated but the questions posed. For, as surely as tock follows tick, if you ask the wrong question you will get the wrong answer. The hedonic psychologists asked 'How happy are you?' when they should have asked 'What is happiness?' As a result, they could do no more than measure and calibrate happiness, and this they did with a precision to rival the anonymous stonema-sons who built the Great Pyramid at Giza. 'Happiness,' as Richard Layard, the United Kingdom's leading happiness economist recently explained,

> can be measured. We can ask people how they feel. We can ask their friends or observers for an independent assessment. Also, remarkably, we can now take measurements of the electrical activity in the relevant part of a person's brain. All of these different measurements give con-sistent answers about a person's happiness.[1]

But what *is* this thing called happiness? The scientists and the social scientists do not stop to ask the question because they presume to know its answer. As a team of eminent psychologists from the American Midwest has spelled out, '[a]ll attempts to comprehend, explain, and predict happiness presuppose that researchers can define [it]'.[2] Presuppose away. Nearly every scientific study allots a single, begrudged paragraph to explaining what happiness actually is. So unencumbered by complexity are these definitions that their articula-tion requires no profusion of words. Happiness is ... well, it's just 'feeling good – enjoying life and wanting the feeling to be main-tained'.[3] So say the economists. In the genial patois of researchers this is called 'subjective well-feeling'. Those now in kindergarten, or who once were, will doubtless be familiar with its romping musical expres-sion, 'If you're happy, and you know it, clap your hands'. Maybe the mystery of happiness has *not* been solved by the palmtop experience sampling. They had the experience but missed the meaning.

Although the psychologists and the economists offered no satisfactory definition of happiness, they did provide, however unwittingly, a vital clue to its whereabouts. In studies of happiness among Maasai tribesmen in Kenya, seal hunters in Greenland and slum dwellers in Calcutta there was one commonality amidst all the diversity. Every study began by declaring, sometimes boasting, that it no longer set store by old ways of thinking that have failed to help us find happiness. Once upon a time, when giants walked the earth, these old ways of thinking were known as philosophy and religion.

In the turf war of happiness, the University of Illinois foot soldiers have planted the banner of psychology in '[what] has historically been the domain of philosophers and theologians'.[4] The economist Richard Easterlin, who commands a platoon from the University of Southern California, reports that '[f]or centuries' – but no longer – 'the contemplation of this desire [happiness] was the exclusive preserve of philosophers and theologians'.[5] And in a bold victory speech from the Netherlands, Ruut Veenhoven, editor of the *Journal of Happiness Studies*, founder of the World Database of Happiness and author of *Correlates of Happiness: 7383 findings from 603 studies in 69 nations, 1991–1994*, decrees that '[c]enturies of philosophical inquiry have failed to result in agreement about what the "good life" is'.[6] Aristotle, for shame!

Still, the battle is not yet lost. We can recover ancient wisdom on happiness and revive traditional notions of the good life. Over the centuries, benefiting from the law of compound intellectual interest, this deposit of wisdom has grown rich and vast. Some ideas about happiness are philosophical, some are religious; some Eastern, some Western; some thousands of years old, some not a hundred. They take the shape of open letters, secret diaries, self-help manuals, logical treatises, sacred scriptures and love poems. They are the wise saws to be tested against modern instances. And such is their vitality that without them life seems wasteful and barren. These ideas are the subject of this book.

Many of the ideas about happiness that appear in the chapters ahead are related to the five world religions: Hinduism, Buddhism, Judaism, Christianity and Islam. This stands to reason, since for most of human history, happiness has been understood, even experienced, in the context of religious belief. Only in the past three or four centuries, and mainly in Western culture, has happiness been divorced, for some people, from faith, religion and spirituality. So here at the outset we find ourselves at what seems to be an impasse: if so many paths to happiness are bound up in religious belief, doesn't that render them invalid for people of other beliefs, or of none? How can a Christian profit from Hindu teachings on happiness? Why should an atheist bother to read the works of Islamic mystics?

In writing this book, I have assumed that the purpose of encountering other religious traditions is not conversion but enlightenment. And that is the spirit in which I invite you to read it. By enlightenment, I mean an appreciative recognition that another's beliefs, traditions or culture can reveal, can offer up, an insight that will enhance one's own beliefs, traditions or culture. Even if we cannot fully enter into someone else's beliefs, still we can learn from them. I suspect that this answer may be unsatisfying to some readers (no doubt because it appears to smack of a politically correct piety), but I believe that if we approach the pursuit of happiness too parochially, we will succeed only in denying ourselves something of value.

Like all great ideas, those about happiness, no matter their origin, flow from minds attuned to universals, minds quickened by concerns basic to our being. For what human creature, even at the risk of a despairing insight, has never inquired into the nature – and possibility – of his or her own happiness? To introduce some of those ideas, I want to tell you the stories of three men who, long ago and far away, in moments of trauma and terrible strain, reflected profoundly about happiness – and then allowed those reflections to suffuse their lives with purpose and meaning. Later, I will expand upon the stories, giving to each its own proper chapter; and I will tell other stories in other chapters, too. For the purposes of this introduction, I want to use them as our preliminary examples, our first glimpses, of what it means to search for happiness. We may not share the lonely burdens of these extraordinary characters, or their ferocious courage, but we are dashed by the same troubles and can be restored by the same consolations.

Epicurus

Epicurus (341–271 BC), if you believe his critics, of whom there have been many throughout history, was a fellow of a most scandalous course of life. Yet even his most aggressive detractors would concede that he was exceptionally clever. A philosopher in ancient Athens, he preached in the city's open marketplace, the *agora*, that the sole source of happiness is pleasure. (The ancient Greek word for pleasure was *hedone*, from which we derive the modern word 'hedonist'.) Pleasure, because it is the key to happiness, must be the ultimate aim of every action: whatever we do, we should do it for pleasure. Epicurus believed that we should embrace pleasure because Nature herself had planted within all of us the desire for it. In a fundamentally healthy way, pleasure was good.

Still, Epicurus preferred to take his pleasures in private. Retreating from society, he founded a quasi-religious cult that survived him by seven centuries and flourished in every part of the Mediterranean world from Herod's Judaea to Caesar's Gaul. It began slowly. Epicurus and his disciples, who wore signet rings bearing his image and committed to memory his precepts and injunctions, retreated to a secret garden outside Athens. There, in splendid isolation, they heeded the call to 'live the obscure life': to renounce luxury, to abstain from sensual indulgence and, most uncharacteristically for inhabitants of democracy's birthplace, to disclaim their civic duties.

But it was the tragic fate of Epicurus to be misunderstood. Partly because his enclave dared to include women – who were politically and intellectually disenfranchised – and partly because it was cut off from the Athenian city-state, outsiders formed a sharply negative picture of this philosophical separatist movement and its mesmerising leader. Epicurus was accused, among other transgressions, of holding orgies with 'Sweet Mama' and 'Baby Lion', the most famous lap-dancers of their day. Six centuries after his death, this 'foul-mouthed bastard', as the Roman philosopher Epictetus branded him, was still being condemned for moral depravity.

Yet the fact of the matter is that Epicureanism, properly understood, promotes none of the self-indulgence and extravagance that have been so detrimentally attributed to it over the centuries. Epicurus, if we look closely, was a generous, reverent and patriotic Athenian. We need only read the man's letters and proverbs (some of which are, bizarrely, preserved in the Vatican) to discover that he taught that the good life requires discipline and restraint.

Once, in all sincerity, he asked his friend Idomeneus to send him a slice of cheese 'so that when I want to have a feast I shall be able to do so'. He claimed that no one's life was ever improved by having an orgasm. He spoke without guile (although his claim must cast into doubt the pride of Baby Lion). Yes, Epicurus believed that pleasure was the secret of happiness; but here's the twist: he defined pleasure not as sensual indulgence – touching this, tasting that – but as the absence of desire. That's where his innumerable critics (Cicero, honourably apart) got him wrong. True pleasure, Epicurus insisted, is marked not by intensity but by tranquillity. Happiness, profound and lasting, is the calm after the storm.

Seneca

In Córdoba, Spain, a few years before the birth of Jesus Christ, was born the greatest expositor of Roman Stoicism. His name was Lucius Annaeus Seneca (4 BC–AD 65). The scion of an established family, he was sent to Rome to be educated and he remained there to pursue a career in government. Despite his advantages, and his eventual prominence, Seneca did not have an easy life.

The emperor Claudius banished him to the island of Corsica (an inhospitable and uncivilised place, where Latin was only rarely heard), mistakenly believing that Seneca had committed adultery with his own niece. Eventually, Seneca was restored to his position at the imperial court, where he exercised vast powers and amassed great riches, under the rule of the next emperor, the infamous Nero. But it was not long before Nero turned his honourable counsellor into a dirty thug. Seneca was forced to plot the assassination of Nero's mother – at Nero's unloving behest – and then to justify the crime before the Senate. Finally, Seneca was ordered to kill himself when the paranoid Nero suspected him of treachery. Though innocent, Seneca had no choice but to do a tyrant's bidding.

In the years of banishment, in the times of upheaval and, finally, in the days before his death, Seneca could not help but wonder why bad things happen to blameless people. If the universe were unjust, how could anyone be sure of finding happiness? The question is grievously perennial. Job, the suffering servant of the Hebrew God, asked much the same. The anguished Seneca, going one step further, answered this seemingly unanswerable question.

Through bombastic and emotionally overwrought adaptations of Greek tragedies, he rendered in dramatic form the abrupt reversals of fortune that visited him over the years. But his most extended reflections, which arose from the pain and misery of his life, are found in his more dignified philosophical writings: dialogues, treatises and personal addresses of consolation and advice to friends and relatives. Faced with impossible moral dilemmas, Seneca took refuge in the Stoic values of detachment and indifference, and found that those values could bring him happiness even in circumstances more dreadful than he could have imagined. Addressing himself as much as his readers, Seneca explained that happiness

> can only be achieved by having, first, a sound mind in constant possession of its soundness; then a brave and energetic mind, which is also gifted with the noblest form of endurance; able to deal with circumstances of the moment; attentive (but not obsessively) to the body and its needs; concerned with other skills that aid our lives, but not too impressed by any of them; using without being a slave to Fortune's gifts ... [E]verlasting freedom and tranquillity follow once we have banished all that vexes and frightens us.[7]

In a spirit of detachment, Seneca calmly awaited a fate whose horrible course he was powerless to alter. Throughout life, his goal had been to harness the mind's rational powers so that he might withstand both the injuries that had been so unfairly and so relentlessly inflicted upon him *and* the seductive charms of good fortune. Emboldened by the Stoic belief that happiness is independent of mere circumstance, he accepted the 'blessings of fortune' without embarrassment or shame, yet remained fully prepared to relinquish them at a moment's notice.[8] When that inevitable moment came – first in exile to Corsica, and later in anxious retirement – he gave up without a struggle every last thing that he possessed, including his own life. But one thing has survived: the pattern of Seneca's noble life, and that belongs to posterity.

Ghazali

In Baghdad, towards the end of the eleventh century, an acclaimed Islamic scholar fell mysteriously ill, renounced his career and spent two years praying alone in a mosque in Damascus. His name was Abu Hamid al-Ghazali (1058–1111). Born in the Persian city of Tûs, Ghazali grew up to be an authority on religious law, in recognition of which he was honoured with the titles 'The Proof of Islam' and 'The Ornament of Faith'. At the young age of thirty-three he was appointed to a professorship at the Nizamiyya college in Baghdad. Shortly after reaching this position of intellectual eminence he fell victim to a debilitating spiritual crisis. It turned out to be the first step in his quest for happiness, a quest that would take him to distant lands over many years.

At the height of his worldly success Ghazali realised, to his shame, that he was too much with the world, too entangled in its strangulating net. He doubted the worth of the subjects he taught and admitted, if only to himself, that his motivation for teaching was the basest of all motives: pride. Firm in his faith, Ghazali knew, nonetheless, that he would be denied eternal life in paradise if he could not discipline his desires and relinquish his attachment to worldly goods. As he lived in fear and indecision, the crisis worsened. One day, standing before his students about to give a lecture, he suddenly lost the power of speech. Soon he could not swallow food. His doctor diagnosed an 'ailment of the heart'. Ghazali, who possessed the soul of a poet, interpreted the clinical findings allegorically: his physical illness was the emblem of his underlying spiritual illness. He stood in danger not of losing his mortal body (that would perish eventually anyway) but of losing something far more precious – his immortal soul.

Just as the crisis was extreme, so was its cure. At the pinnacle of his fame Ghazali abandoned his career, his friends and his wealth. After placing his sons in the care of relatives and leaving money to provide for their education, he travelled to Damascus, where he spent the next two years in reflection and religious devotion. (Geography, alas, prevented the happy coincidence of Ghazali journeying along the same road where, a millennium earlier, St Paul underwent his own conversion.) The minaret in the Umayyad mosque where he prayed in solitude became known as 'the Ghazali minaret'. Through the habit of meditation he became convinced, not in his mind but in his innermost being, that only through direct personal experience could he find the joy that comes from knowing God. Ghazali recovered from his spiritual crisis not through his own strength but through a transcendent one: the light of God shining into his heart.

Ghazali's crisis coincided with his introduction to Sufism, the mystical side of Islam that preaches neither doctrine nor dogma but affirms, above all else, the transforming power of the personal experience of God's presence. The Sufis call this experience *dhawq* – 'taste' – which nicely captures the sensuous immediacy of their vision of happiness. (As the Sufis say, 'he who tastes, knows'.) Surprisingly, this reverence for first-hand experience appealed to a man whose entire life had been devoted to impersonal theories and abstractions. Renouncing, as it were, his confidence in speculative reason, Ghazali vowed to 'walk in the mystic way' so that he might encounter the transcendent wisdom whose only source was direct experience.

What he learned from his conversion to mysticism Ghazali recorded in *The Alchemy of Happiness*, a short book of moral guidance written in Persian for a popular audience. The clue to the secret of happiness lies in the title. Just as the alchemist transforms base metals into precious ones – lead into gold – we can transform our vices into virtues. In the alchemy of happiness we become the best possible version of ourselves, the most precious form of our rough matter.

The lives of Epicurus, Seneca and Ghazali defy, so it seems, nearly every attempt at pattern detection. Certainly, no pattern is detectable in location: a walled garden outside ancient Athens, the court of the emperor Nero and a mosque in Damascus. Spanning fourteen hundred years, these stories encompass classical Greek culture, Rome in its imperial decadence and an Islamic civilisation that stretched from India to Spain. Ghazali alone invokes a specific religious tradition. Epicurus was content to leave the Greek gods on top of Mount Olympus because they were content to ignore what happened below. No doubt Seneca worshipped the Roman equivalent of the Greek deities, but he did not call upon them in his moment of need.

On the face of things, little connects a Greek philosopher with a cult following of prostitutes, a Roman civil servant forced to commit suicide and a Persian scholar who traded books for mystic ecstasy.

But the face of things is not the basis of things. When we look at the world's great thinkers about happiness, we are bound to find them different in time, different in place, different in language and culture. Yet inevitable though these differences are, they cannot obscure the deep similarities in how we search for happiness. The stories of Epicurus, Seneca and Ghazali resonate with us today, thousands of years later, because they are, in truth, our own stories. Within them, we find not enigmatic figures from an alien past but magnified – *magnificent* – versions of ourselves. From these initial examples, these first few accounts of courageous seekers, we can learn some lasting rules about the pursuit of happiness. And that in itself will take us a long way towards clarifying just what the search for happiness means. If we're not clear about that, the searching – and the finding – can never even begin.

Rule #1: *catch big fish*

On a large wooden plaque that hung for many years in my father's study was mounted a fish that he had caught when deep-sea fishing off the Florida coast. It was the biggest one he ever caught, and so it was the only one he ever displayed. Its trophy status was never in jeopardy. The search for happiness is something like that. It's about reeling in the 'big fish' – the only kind that truly matters – even if it means a lot of struggle.

Epicurus, Seneca and Ghazali all fished in deep waters. They shared a commitment to discovering the ultimate ends and purposes of life (the ancients called this *telos*) and they believed in the importance of leading a life that was worthwhile. In different ways, they all reflected upon the shape – the *character* – of their lives as a whole. Out of that reflection dawned the insight that their lives, if they were to be better, would have to change. Epicurus knew that to achieve the tranquillity that would lead to happiness he would have to withdraw from society and seek solace in his pastoral retreat, even though it meant that his reputation was sullied by false allegations of moral depravity. Seneca, instead of raging against injustice or descending into self-pity, turned adversity into triumph by accepting his fate with a calm and tranquil mind. Ghazali, afflicted with an inner torment, recognised that his declining health was a divine summons to cure his sickened soul by embracing a new way of life.

These moments of reckoning all occurred under harrowing conditions: calumny, injustice and emotional collapse. Mercifully, most of us will be spared such torments. That doesn't mean, however, that we don't have our own moments of reckoning; we just have them in ways commensurate with the rest of our lives. While it would be extraordinary for any of us suddenly to quit our job, leave our family and move to a new country, we can still appreciate why a man in Baghdad nearly a thousand years ago felt compelled to do just that. We can empathise with him. In Ghazali's dilemma we recognise a serious version of that psychotherapeutic cliché, the mid-life crisis: the frightening prospect that the life we have so carefully built over the years is without purpose and without value. Far from being a historical curiosity of only passing interest, Ghazali's heroic effort to restore meaning to his life is a distant mirror of our own attempts to straighten out the mess in our lives.

Not too long ago there was a newspaper report about a man who became a millionaire in the lottery yet spent all his winnings in the first year or so, and then got himself arrested on a drugs charge. Clearly this man was no happier despite the short-term pleasure he derived from his financial windfall. The sense of waste that characterises this story ('All that money, and he did *what*?') naturally invites comparison, usually of a self-flattering kind. You might wonder whether such extreme good fortune would make *you* happy. What you have in mind is not the pleasure and enjoyment of winning lots of money (you take that for granted), but rather the way that the money could transform your life. You wonder whether you would have made *better* use of the money. To think like that is to think about the quality of your life as a whole: you understand your life as a series of occasions for taking action and you know that some actions are better than others.

Thinking about life as a whole is intimately tied to making decisions and taking action. When we arrive at the inevitable cross-roads of life we must choose a direction. Do I marry – or forsake – this person? Do I honour – or betray – my friends? Do I tell – or conceal – the truth? We decide such things in light of how we understand our life in its entirety. We think about what we want our life to be like, and then we act accordingly. Everyone's search for happiness demands this kind of big-fish thinking.

Little fish – nice feelings, good moods, raw pleasures – do still matter, only not so much as we might suppose. We all know what obviously happy moments are like; they're the times when everything's great and all that we desire lies within our grasp. Fortunately, there's no end to the experiences that make us feel good: gazing into the eyes of our beloved, scoring the winning goal in a football match, swimming in the ocean (Camus thought this was one of the most intense forms of happiness he had ever known), or being swept up and carried away by a rapturous piece of music. These are the incidents that joyfully crowd a life and make it wonderful. More, please.

But do they make us happy? And if so, how much happiness do they provide? The late philosopher Robert Nozick described pleasurable experiences as 'how life feels from the inside'.[9] He meant, of course, the warmth – the glow – that radiates inside us when we enjoy life. Just think of that eloquent gesture of contemporary self-expression, the air-punch. It's the spontaneous outward sign of irrepressible inward delight. Winning athletes do it when they learn they've won. Talk-show audiences do it when a guest jubilantly confesses, without a whisper of self-reproach, to some barely legal perversion. We've all done it.

Yet no matter how wonderful 'life feels from the inside', such feelings are only the *beginning* of happiness, not its ultimate destination. As Nozick elaborated, we care about many things other than pleasurable experiences. We care about the integrity of our values and beliefs. We care about our accomplishments. We care about leaving a legacy to the world. We care about the well-being of the people in our lives. And, if we're truly magnanimous, we care about the well-being of people *not* in our lives. All these cares bind us to the world – through what we believe, what we achieve and whom we love. This is the ultimately *moral* shape of each person's happiness, and what makes it inseparable from – in truth, dependent upon – the happiness of others. Happiness may, and probably will, begin with pleasurable feelings; but it will also go well beyond them because happiness isn't really about feeling good – it's about being good. The problem is that we are apt to mistake the former for the latter.

It was, ironically, the twentieth century's most influential economist, John Maynard Keynes, who insisted that material prosperity could never confer upon individuals the *purposiveness*, as he called it, that is a necessary part of happiness. In 1928, in a lecture on 'Economic Possibilities for Our Grandchildren', Keynes predicted that when mankind was at last freed from the bondage of poverty and deprivation (a freedom that appeared near on the horizon to the generation between the world wars), it would face the existential challenge of using its material freedom 'to live wisely and agreeably and well'.[10] Who would rise up to meet this challenge? Not the getters and the spenders but those who 'cultivate into a fuller perfection the art of life itself'. Keynes then made the daring leap that some of today's neo-Benthamites and hedonic psychologists are reluctant to make: the leap into the morality of happiness. The 'art of life' consists in being 'more concerned with the remote future results of our actions than with their own quality or their immediate effects on our own environment'.[11] Happiness, that is, means more than pleasing ourselves. It means pleasing others, especially the others we are destined never to know.

Rule #2: wrestle, don't dance

Marcus Aurelius ruled the Roman Empire from 161 to 180 AD, and spent many of those years fighting off foreign invasions in northern Italy and Germany. It was during these harsh military campaigns that Marcus recorded his thoughts in a private document that he titled *To Myself*. Written in Greek, the language of the examined life, the emperor's moral diary is better known to posterity as the *Meditations*. Part of what has ensured that over eighteen centuries this book has never lacked for readers is that its author knew how to turn a phrase. When talking about abstract things, Marcus used lively and unusual images. His favourite one for happiness was wrestling.

A life-long warrior, Marcus certainly spent many hours wrestling since it was one of the dominant aspects of Greco-Roman masculine culture. So, like any good writer, Marcus drew upon his experience. More importantly, though, the choice reveals how Marcus understood happiness. In one of his most insightful passages he explains that happiness feels more like 'wrestling' than 'dancing' because it requires us to 'stand prepared and unshaken to meet what comes and what we did not foresee'. Later in the work, he commanded himself to 'wrestle' to become the kind of man he wished himself to be.

Marcus' words are tough and unforgiving, and they were meant to be. If that old solider had written with more refinement, more delicacy, we wouldn't believe him and he wouldn't have believed himself. It takes a hardness of language to make the hard point that you have to keep working at happiness. You don't just arrive at a blissful destination and then stay there for the rest of your life. Happiness doesn't just happen; it must be prepared for, cultivated and sustained. Over and over again, the match must be re-fought and the victory gained anew.

Perhaps, as his thoughts turned to wrestling, Marcus had been dreaming of Aristotle. For it was the Greek rationalist who had insisted, in his *Nicomachean Ethics*, that we are created for happiness, that it is the ultimate goal of every person's life. But it was also Aristotle who owned up to the disconcerting fact that happiness does not come to us easily. Just as 'one swallow does not make a springtime', he reasoned, one pleasant day does not make a whole life happy. And so in the next breath Aristotle called happiness an *activity*. By this he meant that it requires skill, concentration and focus. Far from being a state of passive enjoyment, like relaxing in a bubble bath or eating a box of chocolates, happiness demands active effort.

Being happy, then, is something that we resolve to achieve rather than something pleasant that comes our way like sunshine after a rainstorm. (The psychologist Mihaly Csikszentmihalyi has similarly argued that the basis of happiness is 'flow', a state of concentration and heightened attentiveness that we make happen within life.) To strive for happiness means not simply that we would like to be happy – who doesn't? – but that we regard our life as a journey in which we move purposefully towards that ultimate goal. Or, to use Marcus' image, becoming happy is like winning a wrestling match.

Epicurus, Seneca and Ghazali all knew something about wrestling for happiness; about winning a better life for themselves in circumstances not in their favour. But even in lives more ordinary we must still wrestle for our happiness. We need only think of moments such as taking a marriage vow (or, indeed, any kind of vow), when we pledge our future and then struggle to honour that pledge. To marry someone is to sign up for a new kind of life in the full – and unsettling – knowledge that this entails renouncing both a former life and all other possible lives. In choosing each other the bride and groom forsake everyone else (for that is what it means to choose), not just for today but for all the tomorrows that they have left together. When couples renew their marriage vows it is not, obviously, because their vows have expired in the way that a library card expires. It is because they wish to rededicate themselves to a union that they cherish even more strongly. The struggle is not a barrier to happiness ('Thank goodness the struggle is over. Now we can dance!'). This is the kind of joyful struggle that *is* happiness.

Rule #3: start at the beginning

Everyone's journey to happiness begins from the same place: unhappiness. We start with the feeling that our lives are out of joint, no matter how stable and fastened they appear. We might be unsure how to repair it, but we sense the misalignment between the life we have and the life we imagine ourselves to have. This is the lovers' quarrel we have with life.

Rarely is our first step towards happiness a giant one. Sometimes we may not even recognise that we are taking it. About five years ago, the journalist David Brooks wrote an amusing book called *Bobos in Paradise*. 'Bobos' means 'Bourgeois Bohemians' – the new elite that emerged out of the dot-com revolution of the 1990s. Brooks argued that, unlike previous generations of successful entrepreneurs, Bobos seek to unite the economic values of capitalism with the social values of the 1960s counterculture. The more Brooks studied Bobos the more he saw the paradox governing their lives: they feel dissatisfied, despite their professional success and material comfort. These evangelists for the gospel of unlimited choice found that they were still searching for something.

On a Sunday afternoon a few months ago I went to a Shaker furniture store. The place was filled with affluent Bobos buying expensive chairs, dressers and tables meant to look simple, homespun and rustic. The customers were trying to connect themselves to the values that the furniture symbolises. They weren't only buying a four-poster bed, they were also buying the *idea* behind the four-poster bed. (Plato would approve.) The purchase was part of the search for what had gone missing in their lives. Of course, you could say this is true of all conspicuous consumption: that we buy things to fill a gap in our lives. Although it takes diverse forms, the Bobo search never varies in content. Colonic irrigation ... rebirthing ... the campaign against genetically modified food: these rather different activities all express the same desire to purify, to be natural, to be authentic.

Of course Bobos are hardly the first people to search for something missing in their lives. The question they face – how do I invest my life with meaning? – is a perennial one. Indeed, it is *the* human question. And behind it lies a general truth about the search for happiness. The truth is that being dissatisfied is a necessary step – the *first* step – towards being happy.

∾

When I set out to explore happiness I didn't know what I would find. That's what it means to explore. But I was pretty sure what I *wouldn't* find. Although it's been possible to derive a few general rules about how to orient the search for happiness, I had no expectation of discovering a grand theory of happiness that applies to everyone in all times and across all cultures. I did not look to find it because I did not think it was there to be found. It would be naive to expect that the Hebrew scriptures, Greek philosophy, the Koran, the Hindu Upanishads and Buddha's Four Noble Truths – to cite just a few works of ancient wisdom about happiness – could be compressed into one single idea about the good life.

'Happy families are all alike,' Tolstoy wrote in the famous first line of *Anna Karenina*. He got it pretty much wrong. The statement 'I am happy' (or 'I am unhappy') carries no *objective* meaning – that is, independent of the person, the subject, making the statement – because it acquires meaning only in a context. Indeed, it must mean something different to every person who utters it. Which explains why all attempts to *measure* happiness are ludicrous, as if it were some massproduced commodity that we could stockpile in times of lazy contentment and then raid in moments of urgent need. (The scientists would, perhaps, insist that *I* am wrong, and Tolstoy right.)

Happiness is less an objective fact to be encountered in the world than an experience to be cultivated by each individual. Thus, we may speak not of any single secret of happiness – applicable to everyone – but only of the *secrets* of happiness – a different one for each person. This is true in an obvious way for people separated by time and place.

The happiness of an ancient Greek cannot be entirely the same as that of a modern Greek (or a modern anybody), just as the happiness of a Muslim cannot be shared by an atheist. And yet each can be happy in his or her way.

Moreover, happiness is never identical even for people united by culture and community. Because individuals face trials and tests that are uniquely theirs, their happiness rises up in a correspondingly unique way. Your happiness belongs to you and to you alone. If we think of happiness as something that we make within life – and not as something that we find elsewhere and then import into life – then we can see, without much difficulty, that any proclamation of happiness must refer back to the individual who proclaims it. So we ought to be less concerned about ironclad definitions, about fitting happiness into precise categories, and more focused on simply making it happen. For although it cannot be deduced theoretically, happiness can be conjured in the moment of experience.

The odd thing about happiness, then, is that this global phenomenon never acts on the world stage, but only ever makes local appearances. So while there is no unchanging idea of happiness the term itself encompasses a range of meanings, some of which are bound to be inconsistent. A concept of happiness that appears natural to one culture or historical moment may appear alien to another. Indeed, some versions of happiness are simply irreconcilable: Stoics train themselves to rely on reason while religious mystics free themselves from reason's shackle; Utilitarians insist on maximising pleasure while Buddhists strive to suppress desire. Not all approaches to happiness are equally practical: Hinduism places a strong emphasis on the duties and responsibilities of everyday life, while Christianity emphasises that we cannot become truly happy on our own because we need the gift of God's grace. Yet the differences arise not because the paths to happiness are insufficient or incomplete (those demerits belong, unfortunately, to *us*), but because being different is part of what it means to belong to your own culture and to exist in your own time.

Still, there is unity in diversity. The differences do not fall beyond the circumference of our understanding. Every conception of the good life that has emerged throughout history, in whatever culture, takes up the same four themes: pleasure, desire, reason and suffering. These are the irreducible elements of happiness, its fundamental shape, its indelible texture. These are the things we reckon with as we strive to find happiness. But we reckon with them in a particular way: to be happy we must be able to moderate pleasure, to control desire, to transcend (or rely upon) reason and to endure suffering. The examples in this introduction begin to show us how the reckoning takes place. Epicurus picked his pleasures carefully, and so controlled his desires; Seneca used reason's strength to protect him from adversity; Ghazali found the hidden meaning that lies beyond reason. In the chapters ahead we will look at still further examples of how we can create happiness in the circumstances of life as we live it here and now.

Be they ancient or modern, Eastern or Western, religious or secular, all visions of happiness focus on these few enduring existential dilemmas, and differ only in the manner, marvellously kaleidoscopic, of mixing and applying them. These multiple visions do not betray any weakness in happiness but consecrate its power, like that of some fantastical yet benevolent shape-shifter, to suit the exigencies of the time.

If we listen to the wisdom of the ages, we will hear, faintly at first, and then ever more loudly, a single and sustained refrain. Played in different keys and tuned to different pitches, but still, and always, the same resounding chords. Should we be disappointed that, unlike the universe, happiness does *not* expand infinitely? Let us instead rejoice that happiness may well be the one thing that can resist unpredictability. For however happiness arises in our life, it must do so within the context of perennial, not accidental, let alone unexpected, concerns; whatever it is about, it is about a few constant things: pleasure, desire, reason and suffering. The secrets to happiness lie here, and nowhere else.

You probably will not read this book to absorb vast amounts of history, philosophy and theology (although it is there for the absorp-tion-minded). You will read it, more likely, to be inspired by the greatest ideas in history about happiness. Such a yearning led me to write it. So my hope is that you will use it to reflect upon the project of your life; to ask yourself, unblinkingly, whether you are leading the good life; to become, in short, the architect of your own happiness.

Part I
Living for Pleasure

1

Maximise Your Pleasure (The Utilitarians)

The eighteenth-century English legal philosopher Jeremy Bentham unveiled his hyper-rational theory of happiness in a monumental work of jurisprudence for which he wrote the introduction but nothing else. We cannot charge the man with laziness, since the introduction ran to more than 300 pages. Still, Bentham was reluctant to publish it, knowing that he was capable of even more. His less cautious friend, George Wilson, a Scottish barrister, urged him to have the essay printed without delay, because a rival scholar's impending publication threatened to make Bentham's own work redundant. Moreover, drafts of his other essays were already in circulation, and it would not be long before some enterprising but unscrupulous scholar stole his ideas. At last Bentham agreed, warily, that his 'dry and tedious' work should be set before the public.[1] By this time, however, the rats that infested Bentham's modest law chambers had begun to devour the original manuscript. The author quickly rescued his work, bundled it off to the printer and promptly published the uneaten portions as *An Introduction to the Principles of Morals and Legislation* (1791).

The title is misleading, for the book is not a study of morals and legislation; it is, rather, an almanac of crime and punishment. (Bentham, who spent a lot of time thinking about criminals, designed a prison where all inmates could be placed under constant surveillance. Commissioned, but rejected, by Parliament, it was called the

Panopticon, Greek for 'all seeing'.) Oddly – although the oddity is but a seeming one – Bentham's book on crime and punishment is his lasting contribution to the pursuit of happiness, for in its pages he explains how we can attain happiness through rationally chosen pleasures. Bentham's dreary name for the pleasure principle was *utility*, a word that in his day connoted not usefulness, but satisfaction: when an object 'produce[s] benefit, advantage, pleasure, good, or happiness' – words that for Bentham were all synonyms.[2] Rationality is the key to understanding why utilitarian theory remains so powerfully attractive: because it explains happiness logically, clearly and completely. For every question, Bentham's model provides an answer.

To the question 'How do we measure happiness?', Bentham answered with something of his own invention: the 'felicific calculus', or happiness equation. But who shall perform the calculus? Who crunches the happiness numbers? For Bentham, the answer was obvious: the government. Bentham's primary concern was the social environment in which we all strive to maximise our utility (or pleasure) and thus increase our happiness. *How* anyone should pursue happiness was best left to the individual concerned. Still, somebody has to ensure that the pursuit is possible in the first place – and that is government's job: to create the conditions that allow all of us to seek happiness in whatever way we feel best. So Bentham wrote his *Introduction* with politicians in mind (hence, the numbing bureaucratic tone), and he was keen to give them everything they needed to know about happiness so that they could pass laws to promote it.

That, beyond question, is the profound and lasting influence of utilitarianism upon how we today think of happiness: that it is not undertaken in isolation but always through contact with other people, always in the civic arena. And so the pursuit can be helped or hindered by that meddling creature called government.

'The greatest happiness'

In the year that Thomas Jefferson wrote 'the pursuit of happiness' into the founding document of American liberty, Bentham, on the other side of the Atlantic, committed himself to the principle of 'the greatest happiness of the greatest number'. What Bentham meant, first of all, was that the rightness (or wrongness) of an action depends entirely upon its *consequences*, and neither upon the action itself nor the motives of the actor. The rule of thumb is this: in any circumstance, the morally right action is the one that produces the best outcome. The best outcome is the one that 'augment[s] the happiness of the community'.[3] For Bentham, the more happiness an action produces, the more preferable it becomes.

Though he took an inclusive approach to happiness, Bentham still defined it in traditionally hedonistic terms: maximising pleasure and minimising pain. Indeed, he begins the *Introduction* by asserting that pleasure and pain 'govern us in all we do, in all we say, in all we think'.[4] It's hard to imagine a statement more sweeping than that. Since pleasure controls 'all we do', it cannot be merely passive contentment or submissive enjoyment; rather, it must involve action, deliberate and overt. Pleasure, then, is volitional: what we *will* to do. (This meaning is not entirely foreign to us, since the word 'pleasure' still carries a residual sense of intention. In Britain prisoners are said to be detained 'at Her Majesty's pleasure' not because the Queen enjoys throwing people into jail but because she *wills* their imprisonment, as the proper punishment for their crimes.) Also, pleasure is absolute. There is no greater goal than pleasure, nor anything other than pleasure that we would strive to obtain. It's not as if you prefer to maximise pleasure while I prefer justice, or perhaps charity. No, we *all* want pleasure and we want it *all the time*.

By *community*, Bentham meant not an idea or abstraction divorced from the desires and experiences of actual people but, quite simply, an aggregate of individuals. Because only individuals experience pleasure and pain, only they (strictly speaking) can be happy. Thus, the community's happiness is nothing but the sum total of the happiness experienced by the people who comprise it: you and me and everybody we know. So when we say that a community is happy, we are saying that most of the people within it are happy. That is why Bentham referred to the community as a 'fictitious body': because it is just convenient shorthand for a group of individuals.[5]

Still, the community matters. Provided that our actions do not affect others, we are at liberty to do whatever maximises our pleasure and minimises our pain. But when our actions *do* affect others, then we must stop to consider the probable consequences and tailor our behaviour accordingly. (This is the idea behind the colloquial expression 'Your right to throw a punch ends at the tip of my nose'.) In all circumstances, we must choose the action that is most likely to increase pleasure for the *group as a whole* – and sometimes that will require us to sacrifice our immediate happiness in order to secure a greater happiness for our friends and neighbours. Disagreeable though it must be to prodigal sons and daughters everywhere, the 'greatest happiness' principle tells us that our own desire for pleasure matters no more than anyone else's.

The catalogue of pleasure

Anyone who believes that happiness consists in securing more pleasure than pain ought to have an encyclopaedic knowledge on the matter. To such knowledge Bentham aspired, and his zeal for tabulating, organising and classifying data is nowhere more apparent than in the *Introduction*, where he offers an impressively detailed account of pleasures and pains, their sources, their variations and our motives for attaining or avoiding them. In a phrase that now strikes an unintended note of lechery, he called it his 'catalogue of pleasure'.

Apart from its slightly archaic language, Bentham's roster reads just as we would expect: 'wealth', 'power' and 'skill' rank high among the pleasures, while 'privation', 'enmity' and 'awkwardness' – their opposites – are the chief pains. Merely to glance at Bentham's hedonic inventory is to recognise that he permitted only quantitative (*more* and *less*) distinctions between pleasures. Qualitative distinctions (*better* and *worse*) had no standing. Thus, as long as the resulting quantity of pleasure was the same, the child's game of 'pushpin', he declared, was just as good as 'poetry'. A blunt egalitarianism is at work here: equal amounts of pleasure are equally worthwhile, no matter their source. Whether it be throwing darts, composing sonnets or torturing kittens (some people *do* like that sort of thing), no one kind of pleasure is intrinsically superior to another.

Crunching the numbers

To know whether we are as happy as we can be, Bentham devised his 'felicific calculus'. Put simply, *happiness equals pleasure minus pain.* Of course, it is misleading to state matters so simply, especially when it took Bentham hundreds of pages to explain the equation's hidden intricacies. The first step in calculating happiness is to weigh all the pleasures and pains in our life. This is more complicated than just putting them on a scale (what would that scale look like?) since we need to know various things about them: their aspects, the circum-stances affecting them and how they relate to each other. To begin with the aspects: 'intensity', 'duration', 'certainty', 'propinquity', 'fecundity', 'purity' and 'extent'. These are the factors that determine *how much* pleasure or pain arises from a given action.

The aspects are more commonsensical than they seem. Intensity and duration are the basic properties of all pleasures and pains: a certain force (intensity) exerted over a certain time (duration). We must also, however, account for pleasures and pains that have yet to occur because we do have anticipatory feelings about them, whether looking forward to a vacation or fearing the dentist's drill. In consid-ering future pleasures and pains, we assign a value to both their likeli-hood (certainty) and their timeframe (propinquity). The more certain you are to be promoted, for example, the more pleasure you will derive from thinking about it; and as the date of your advancement draws nearer, the more excited you become.

We must also have regard for fecundity and purity, the knock-on effects of pleasure and pain. Fecundity, or fruitfulness, refers to the likelihood that a sensation will duplicate itself: that pleasure will beget more pleasure, or pain more pain. Purity, however, refers to the likelihood that a sensation will *not* be followed by its opposite, but rather will remain its own 'pure' self – pleasure will not lead to pain, nor pain give rise to pleasure. Finally, we must determine how much our pleasures and pains affect others. To employ Bentham's term, we want to know their 'extent'. When parents take pride in their children's achievements, or suffer sympathetically when they fall ill, the initial pleasure or pain extends outward to them, like ripples spreading across a lake.

In short, Bentham is telling us to ask the following questions to determine the value of any given pleasure or pain:

- How forceful is it? (intensity)
- How long will it last? (duration)
- How likely is it to occur? (certainty)
- How soon will it occur? (propinquity)
- Will it lead to more of itself? (fecundity)
- Will it not lead to its opposite? (purity)
- How much does it affect other people? (extent)

He also penned a few lines to remind readers of these same aspects of pleasure and pain:

Intense, long, certain, speedy, fruitful, pure –
Such marks in pleasures and in pains endure.
Such pleasures seek, if private be thy end:
If it be public, wide let them extend.
Such pains avoid, whichever be thy view:
If pains must come, let them extend to few.[6]

Let's put this theory to work. Suppose that you want to know how much happiness you derive from gardening. First, you assign a value to each relevant pleasure: the satisfaction of achievement, the tranquillity of the work, the warmth of the sun and, of course, the beauty of the flowers themselves. Then you add them up to determine the sum total of the pleasure you take in gardening. Next, you follow the same procedure but with respect to each pain: blistered hands, stiff knees, bee stings, the bothersome sight of weeds and the toxic fumes of insect repellant. Finally, you subtract the total value of pain from the total value of pleasure. The sum left over is your happiness (or unhappiness). If the final number is greater than zero, then you are happy, and the higher the number the happier you are. Keep on planting. But if your balance is negative, then you are unhappy, and the greater the deficit the more profound your misery. Put down the trowel now.

For simplicity's sake, I have left out something important: the *effect* that your garden has on other people. (Bentham called this the 'extent' of pleasure.) Because, like all of us, you seek the greatest happiness of the greatest number, you can't get away with saying that *you* derive pleasure from gardening, and nobody else matters. Other people *do* matter, and in their collectivity they matter more than you do. So the real question becomes: does your garden make the *community* happy? To figure that out you must go back and repeat all the pleasure and pain calculations for all the people who have witnessed your handiwork. True, these calculations will become increasingly complex if people have different reactions to your garden (they love it, they hate it), you are unable to determine their reactions (they don't tell you), or you don't know how many people to factor into the equation (so many have walked by that you've lost track). Yet only by performing these calculations can you know with certainty how much happiness your actions create for the entire community.

It is reassuring to pursue happiness in a rational and ordered way; the logic of it makes us believe that the pursuit will be successful, if only we turn our minds to it. Happiness, when so carefully explained, seems achievable – which is certainly what we all want. Bentham understood, however, that we could not, each of us, spend so much time calculating the odds for happiness that we never get around to doing the things that actually make us happy. In fact, he never imagined that the general public would use the 'felicific calculus'. Rather, he intended it to be a tool for politicians, to help them pass laws to maximise general levels of happiness. As Bentham explained, the calculus's true purpose is legislative: to apportion happiness throughout the community (rather like Santa Claus distributing toys). Leaving to the politicians all these intricate rules, complex formulae and unwieldy calculations, we can get on with simply being happy.

Legislating happiness

In Bentham's view, we should entrust the government with our happiness, but not because we are too lazy to secure it for ourselves. (Is anyone that apathetic about their own welfare?) Rather, we confer this responsibility upon the state because it can do the job better, certainly in the narrow sense of ensuring that we are free to pursue our desires without obstruction or interference. Bentham's view strikes a pleasing balance: on the one hand, the state wants us to be happy; on the other hand, it won't micro-manage the process.

From the political theorists of the English Civil War – Thomas Hobbes, author of *Leviathan* (1651), most notably – Bentham inherited the belief that governments exist to form stable and peaceful civil societies as the best alternative to the state of nature. No blissful Garden of Eden, the state of nature is chaos that soon descends into the 'war of all against all' (*bellum omnia omnes*) as everybody tries to satisfy their desires at everybody else's expense. Because no one can be happy in such dreadful circumstances (Hobbes famously warned that life in the state of nature was 'nasty, brutish and short'), we surrender our natural rights to form a governed peaceful society in which everybody's odds of finding happiness are greatly improved. To gain a lot of security, we give up a little freedom. Thus, the sole purpose of government is to give us what we all want but cannot achieve on our own: happiness.

But those who govern need to be taught how, and Bentham appointed himself their tutor. Not even the most tireless lawmaker, however, could possibly determine *all* the actions required to maximise the happiness of *all* the people. Happiness must be achieved at something faster than a snail's pace. Bentham's advice to politicians was that if they got the big things right then all the little things would fall into place. Getting the big things right means protecting each citizen's life and property: you cannot be happy if your life is endangered or your property at risk. Indeed, you would gladly spend the time and incur the expense necessary to prevent risk or harm to either. *That* is the responsibility of government, and the reason you sacrificed some of your natural liberty to create it in the first place. So we now have a definition of good government: one that allows you to sleep easily at night, trusting that your throat will not be slit, your daughter will not be raped and your house not set on fire. (We expect governments to do more than that – for example, to provide for us when we are old and sick—but we are speaking now of minimum requirements.) By safeguarding your life and property, the state grants you the freedom to pursue happiness.

Bentham called this freedom 'security', and he believed that without it no one could be happy. But freedom has its limits – the state neither forces you to pursue happiness (you are free to be unhappy) nor dictates which actions will help you to find it (you must determine that for yourself). Each person, as Bentham says, must 'direct his own conduct to the production of his own happiness'.[7] The state contributes to that endeavour by making sure that nothing obstructs you on your journey, so to speak. But what that journey entails – choices you make, actions you undertake, relationships you form, goals you set – is for you to decide. The government will intervene only if your pursuit of happiness obstructs someone else's. This is called *probity*: the state uses punishment, both threatened and actual, to stop us from harming each other; from making each other unhappy.

Now we see more clearly why Bentham's treatise on happiness is really a handbook of crime and punishment: because crime (more than anything else) diminishes our happiness and punishment (more than anything else) guarantees the 'security' that is its foundation. Perverse as it seems, only by implementing a rational system of coercion – throwing people into jail – can the state promote the happiness of its citizens. Indeed, Bentham was convinced that the loss of happiness (or its opposite, the creation of unhappiness) was the sole basis for punishing criminals. The more a crime 'disturbs' happiness, he believed, the more 'demand it creates for punishment'.[8] Thus, a man who steals £100 from a poor person deserves a harsher sentence than a man who steals the same from a rich person because he has inflicted comparatively greater misery upon his impecunious victim. He has, in effect, stolen *more* happiness.

Roadblocks to happiness

Bentham makes a winning first impression. Staunch rationalists that we are, and believers in scientific inquiry, we approve of such a comprehensive approach to the good life. In utilitarianism we find a universal model fit for purpose: all people, in all circumstances, can apply the model to determine – indeed, to bring about – their own happiness.

But when we take a closer look, the flaws in Bentham's theory of happiness start to appear. Suddenly, there are wrinkles, creases and grey hairs that had escaped our notice in an earlier moment of infatuation. For starters, the 'felicific calculus', no matter who uses it, does not work all that smoothly. It lacks units of measurement, and you cannot measure anything without a scale, whether inches and feet, ounces and pounds, or quarts and gallons. What, exactly, is the unit of measurement for happiness? The *happino*? Yet even if such a scale existed, it would be inadequate because no single unit of measurement can express both force and duration, which are the most basic aspects of how we feel our pleasures and pains. The pleasure of an orgasm is both intense and brief, but not 'intense/brief'. The pleasure of reading a favourite novel is not 'moderate/long'. We do not speak of pleasure in such a way. And yet if we cannot calibrate differences of force and duration, then we cannot determine a final sum of happiness. We cannot quantify happiness with even the remotest precision.

We may also come to doubt Bentham's view that pleasure is the sole and unerring basis of happiness. Going back to his catalogue of pleasure, we find something surprising: that 'malevolence' appears as both a pain *and* a pleasure. How can this be? Surely, malevolence – wickedness, evildoing – must count only as a pain, because it entails suffering. True, Bentham would say; but that is only how the victim sees it. A malevolent person *enjoys* someone else's suffering, whether he inflicts it or merely rejoices at its occurrence. Pleasurable malevolence is not limited to arch/criminals, for who does not quietly smile when an irritating colleague says something stupid in a meeting? In any act of malevolence, large or small, whatever pains the victim pleases the oppressor – and so creates happiness for him, if not for anyone else. Bentham does not shy away from that conclusion.

But we probably do shy away. Probably we want to condemn malevolent pleasures and deny that they could make anyone happy. Yet within the rules of Bentham's game – all pleasures are created equal – we cannot make such a move. (Pushpin is as good as poetry.) Bentham gives us no rational basis for claiming that some pleasures are bad, even though our conscience tells us this must be so. That is an important insight about the pursuit of happiness: even if we embrace pleasure as the very substance and basis of a happy life, we feel that something *other* than pleasure must also be factored in. Mere pleasure cannot be the foundation of a worthy life. So while the attractions of utilitarian thought are undeniable – the logic, the clarity, the got/it/all/figured/out confidence – we must temper the attraction by recog/nising that happiness has a dimension beyond pleasure; and this extra dimension – call it conscience, morality or good character – must be given its due.

Is everybody happy?

Nor, to focus upon a further drawback, is it clear whether 'the greatest happiness' principle guarantees that everyone will become happy. The confusion lies in the phrase itself. Initially, Bentham seems to have had in mind the overall amount of happiness – the *quantum*, as he called it – rather than its distribution within the community. This blunt *quantum* served an equally blunt purpose: to ensure that the majority enjoyed as much happiness as possible (and to hell with everybody else). Whether the majority was slim or overwhelming didn't matter, just as it didn't matter whether the minority was mildly discontent or in abject despair. The *only* thing that mattered was that the majority maximised its happiness.

In the happiness lottery – it's that random – we all stand an equal chance of winning. And the chances are pretty good, since more than fifty per cent of us ('the greatest number') will end up happy. But while most of us are guaranteed to win, a few are bound to lose. We accept this disparity in outcome because the contest itself is fair: nobody has a head start; nobody is more likely to become happier than anyone else; and nobody can predict the outcome. As Bentham insisted, 'each [person] is to count for one and no one for more than one'.[9] The duke and his gamekeeper both have an equal claim to happiness. Utilitarianism thus satisfies our commitment to fair play, not because it guarantees equal outcomes (it doesn't) but because it ensures equal opportunities.

But fairness comes at a price, and that price is brutality. In order for most people to be happy, a few *must* be unhappy. They may be woefully unhappy, or even forced into slavery – whatever it takes for the majority to maximise its own happiness. This is the infamous 'tyranny of the majority': the many are free to do whatever they want to the few. (In *Democracy in America*, Alexis de Tocqueville warned that the systematic oppression of the minority by the majority was democracy's dark side.) Bentham, though no champion of individual moral rights, did try to mitigate the harsh consequences of utilitarian ethics. It worried him greatly that his own principles might justify – worse, bring about – the oppression of the unhappy few by the happiness-hungry many.

Gradually, he realised that the 'greater number' of people must be prevented from tyrannising the 'lesser number' – even if it *lowered* the overall amount of happiness in the community. Towards the end of his career, in the late 1820s, Bentham defended a more equitable distribution of happiness, which he called 'the greatest happiness maximised'. Inequities would be corrected by transferring some of the majority's happiness to the minority. That way, the happiness scales would be more balanced, and *everyone's* happiness – not just the lucky lottery winners' – would be secured.

No longer hopeless

If ever a child were raised to be the test case for Bentham's strict principles, it was the moral philosopher John Stuart Mill (1806–73). His father, James, a utilitarian and political radical, groomed his son from an early age for the commanding role he was to play in Britain's intellectual life. Precociously, the seven-year-old read Plato's dialogues – in the original Greek. A year or two later, having mastered Latin, he took on Virgil, Horace, Livy and Ovid. As an adolescent he turned to the study of natural sciences and law, reading Isaac Newton and Adam Smith.

Forbidden to attend university (although hardly short on knowledge), Mill took up a post at the East India Company alongside his father, who had secured the boy's appointment on the day after his seventeenth birthday. He eventually rose to the high-level position of Chief Examiner, and remained at the Company until it was dissolved in 1858. In those days, when it took months for dispatches to arrive on steamships from Bombay, there wasn't much to occupy a clerk's time in the office of the Examiner of India Correspondence. So Mill was free to devote half the day to his own, more voluminous, writings – or, as he called them, his 'private intellectual pursuits'.[10]

At first, the young Mill was an ardent disciple of utilitarianism, praising it as the 'keystone which held together the detached and fragmentary component parts of my knowledge'.[11] For eighteen months he served as Bentham's secretary, and struggled to transcribe the great man's rambling pronouncements. All that changed in 1827, when, barely out of his teens, Mill suffered what he called a 'crisis in his mental history'. We would call it a nervous breakdown. He complained of a 'dull state of nerves' that made him 'unsusceptible to enjoyment or pleasurable excitement'.[12] The company of friends gave him no joy and the privacy of books no relief. He could only stand by and watch as the 'whole foundation on which [his] life was constructed fell down'.[13]

The turnaround came suddenly, as these things often do, when he was reading Jean-François Marmontel's *Mémoires*. When he came to the passage where the youth Marmontel confronts the reality of his father's death, Mill, to his astonishment, took on the character's sorrow and began to weep. This from a man who knew nothing but discipline and drill, restriction and rote. The teardrops that moistened the pages of his book were the longed-for sign that he 'was no longer hopeless', no longer an unfeeling 'stone'.[14] As the gloomy clouds lifted, Mill rejoiced to discover that he still possessed 'some of the material out of which all worth of character, and all capacity for happiness, are made'.[15]

A generation and more of Freudian psycho-biographers have had a field day with this story, reading it as a classic Oedipal narrative of the son's subconscious desire to kill his father. There is some truth in that, for Mill's depression must have stemmed partly from repressed hostility towards an overbearing and emotionally indifferent parent upon whom he was entirely dependent. (After his father's death, nine years later, Mill developed a permanent twitch in his right eye.) But that is not how Mill himself wrote about the episode in a work that does not lack for unembarrassed candour. Rather, he understood his 'crisis' to be a turning point in his view of happiness.

Poetry did the turning. Some months later, when he read Wordsworth for the first time, Mill finally liberated himself from the 'reasoning machine' of Bentham's cold-hearted logic. Enraptured though he was by Wordsworth's evocations of nature and nature's beauty, Mill looked upon the poetry as 'medicine for [his] state of mind' because it imparted to him 'the perennial sources of happiness, when all the greater evils of life shall have been removed'.[16] With those hopeful words, Mill gave to the story of his life a familiar Romantic theme: the triumph of imagination over reason. Reason, because it breaks things down into parts, allows us to understand their structure; but imagination, because it integrates, allows us to grasp their meaning. And it was meaning that Mill was after.

Embracing poetical culture – and its openness to emotion – led Mill to revise his view of happiness. Like Bentham, he continued to believe that happiness was the ultimate purpose of life, and that it was bound up in pleasure and pleasurable experiences. But he formed a different idea about how to achieve it. The secret of happiness, he realised, was the paradox that you find it only by searching for something else. Happy people are those

> who have their minds fixed on some object other than their own happiness; on the happiness of others, on the improvement of mankind, even on some art or pursuit, followed not as a means, but as itself an ideal end. Aiming thus at something else, they find happiness by the way.[17]

The many sides of life

This was like throwing cold water over Bentham's head. In claiming that we find happiness indirectly – 'by the way' – Mill was explicitly rejecting Bentham's mechanistic view of human nature. Utility may well be the primary motive for all human behaviour (we all seek pleasure), but human beings cannot be reduced to machines that make rational – and *only* rational – calculations about it. There are 'many things', Mill wrote, 'which [utilitarian] doctrine ... ought to have made room for, and did not'.[18] There is something within us that exceeds reason, escapes logic, and Mill faulted Bentham for neglecting this 'many-sided' nature of human life.[19]

Yet Mill himself was the product of this same neglect, for the art of life had been categorically excluded from the highly regimented and solitary education that he had received from his father. (Horseback riding and hiking, yes; but other than scraps from Shakespeare, no poetry.) The exclusion had unfortunate consequences, since it put beyond the boy's reach all the feelings, experiences and attitudes that, as a man, he understood to be the very heart of a life that was worthwhile. This is where Mill began to reshape the utilitarian idea of happiness, and rescued it from being nothing more than a favourable ratio of pleasure to pain.

Happiness demands that we develop a 'sense of honour', a 'love of beauty' and a 'love of order', Mill said.[20] The ultimate purpose of life is not to make blunt calculations of utility but to become a better person. (It sounds very modern to say that happiness is related to self-improvement, but actually it is one of the oldest ideas in Western culture for it dates back to Aristotle, who taught that we 'grow' into happiness like a sapling that grows into a tree.) Even as Mill acknowledged that the controlling environment of his youth had stunted his character development, he insisted that no person was a prisoner to his upbringing. With effort, *anyone* could alter his character for the better, and education's purpose was to make the betterment happen. As Mill knew firsthand from the therapeutic power of Wordsworth's poetry, aesthetic education provides one excellent opportunity for self-improvement. But learning a lesson from poetry requires imagination, the very thing that Bentham had so prejudicially cast aside.

In coming around to this view, Mill set himself the challenge of uniting the utilitarian pursuit of happiness-through-pleasure with a classical concern for the good life. Somehow, he had to show that maximising utility was the right way to become a *better* person (in the way that Aristotle had meant) and not just a person who enjoyed more pleasure for pleasure's sake (in the way that Bentham had meant). The cornerstone of this new argument was the recognition that pleasures differed in *quality* as well as *quantity*. Some pleasures are better than others, and the better pleasures are the ones we should pursue; the ones that will make us truly happy.

Pigs and fools and the quality of pleasure

'It is quite compatible with the principle of utility to recognise the fact, that some kinds of pleasure are more desirable and more valuable than others.'[21] It is 'absurd', Mill continued in his famous essay *Utilitarianism* (1861), to suppose that the 'estimation of pleasures' should depend on 'quantity alone'.[22] But how do we tell higher pleasures from lower ones? Partly by who experiences them. The lowest pleasures – food, drink, defecation and sex – entail mere physical sensation, and so are experienced by humans and animals alike. The highest pleasures – reason, imagination and moral sentiment – rely upon thought, and so are enjoyed only by humans. Moreover, we deem lower pleasures inferior because they are short-lived and require neither effort nor skill (a hungry person does not need to be taught the pleasure of eating). By contrast, higher pleasures are more enduring and do require effort and skill (we need to be taught how to play a Beethoven sonata). So the way to be happy is to pick our pleasures carefully.

We prize the highest pleasures precisely because they involve uniquely human faculties, and thus are the sign and testament of our superior place in nature's hierarchy. The more a pleasure is exclusively human, said Mill, the higher it is, and the more assiduously we should pursue it. This is a familiar argument – 'Go for the gold', as the modern Olympians cry – and one that appeals to the vanity of our species. For us, nothing but the best. As rational actors, we know that the best pleasures are intellectual, not sensual, and so we privilege the mind over the body.

But make no mistake: no puritans are we. To aim exclusively for the high intellectual pleasures is no hardship because, as Mill argues, no one 'really wish[es] to sink into what he feels to be a lower grade of existence'.[23] If we *did* wish to slide into a debased form of life, then we would no longer be human; we would be animals. But we are not animals, not any more. Having broken through the evolutionary ceiling, we are not about to fall back down, especially when it has taken so many thousands of generations to get to where we now are.

When Mill's contemporary, the historian Thomas Carlyle, denounced utilitarianism as a 'pig philosophy', he meant that its emphasis on pleasure reduced human beings to the base level of animals. If happiness entailed only the gratification of desire, Carlyle warned, then happiness was hardly worth having. Rolling in mud and sticking your snout in a trough could not possibly count as living the good life. Unless, of course, you were a pig – and then it was very good, indeed.

The flaw in Carlyle's argument, at least from Mill's perspective, was his assumption that humans and pigs enjoy the same pleasures. That is true, but only partially so. All creatures go forth and multiply, but only we humans compose sonnets and paint pictures about it. Thus, in his memorable riposte to Carlyle, Mill declared that

> [i]t is better to be a human being dissatisfied than a pig satisfied; better to be Socrates dissatisfied than a fool satisfied. And if the fool, or the pig, is of a different opinion, it is because they only know their own side of the question. The other party to the comparison knows both sides.[24]

In others words, pigs and fools don't know what they're missing. Which is what makes them pigs and fools in the first place. But we who are wise, we who know 'both sides' of the question, can distin⟨

guish piggy pleasures from Socratic ones. What makes one pleasure superior to another is the 'nobleness of character' – courage, nobility, dignity, duty or self-sacrifice – that it demands. These virtues are what really matters about pleasure, and are the very reason we pursue it: to possess its desirable attributes, so that we might acquire a noble character.

The daisy chain of happiness

Eager to prove that the utilitarian vision of happiness was altruistic, not selfish, Mill tried to reconcile the seemingly incompatible goals of the individual ('what *I* want') and the group ('what *they* want'). His resolution was mutuality: any one person's happiness depends upon everyone else's. Thus, you cannot be happy unless your neighbours are, just as they cannot be unless you are. We are still motivated by the desire to maximise our own happiness; but we come to realise that this desire can be fulfilled only indirectly. If you look after someone else, someone else will look after you, and everyone will look after each other in a daisy chain of happiness. And if a person of noble character is not always the happier for his nobility, 'there can be no doubt that it makes other people happier, and that the world in general is immensely a gainer by it'.[25]

We must secure other people's happiness first – because that is the only way to guarantee ours – and we must look upon ourselves as a 'disinterested and benevolent spectator'.[26] From this new detached perspective, we see that our desires are no more important, no more urgent, than anyone else's. No greater necessity attaches itself to my happiness than to yours, and so I will always treat you with the same care and concern that I would naturally bestow upon myself. So wholeheartedly did Mill believe that utilitarian ethics required total regard for others that he compared it, unabashedly (outrageously, some might say), to Christianity:

In the golden rule of Jesus of Nazareth, we read the complete spirit

45

of the ethics of utility. To do as one would be done by, and to love one's neighbour as oneself, constitutes the ideal perfection of utilitarian morality.[27]

But let us not be so quick to preach. Suppose that, in my moment of ideal perfection, I sacrifice my happiness for yours. Mind you, my sacrifice is not good in itself – virtue is *not* its own reward – but good only to the extent that it makes you happy (and, as a bonus, maybe a few others, too). Not exactly selfless, my sacrifice is a rationally calculated investment – do not call it noble – which I expect will yield a high rate of return. If I thought the sacrifice was a bad investment, I wouldn't make it. So, contrary to the gospel's spirit, the left hand *does* know what the right one is doing. But results matter most. If my sacrifice makes other people happy, then it will have been worthwhile, because in the long run it will make me happy, too. But if it fails – if no one becomes happier – then my efforts will have been 'wasted' (that's Mill's word), and I would have been better off just looking after myself – and myself alone.[28]

Resist the dark side

Why do so many of us find utilitarianism morally repugnant? After all, it aims to make most people happy. Yet we already know the objections: people can derive happiness (in principle) from actions that most of us regard as immoral; the majority is free to tyrannise the minority; and individual moral rights are left unprotected. Utilitarianism makes us pay a staggeringly high price for our happiness.

The rigidity of Bentham's scheme troubled Mill, who tried to overcome it by appealing to 'the art of life' and the 'nobleness of character' that have nothing to do with maximising pleasure. In effect, he made something other than pleasure the basis for action, and so made a distinction between things we *do* and things we *should do*. He was, in effect, saying, 'we should seek pleasure not for itself, but only for some aspect of it that we regard as valuable'. Mill had to follow this curved line of reasoning because otherwise he could not have claimed, as he did, that a small quantity of a higher pleasure (say, a few minutes reading Wordsworth) counts for more than a large quantity of a lower pleasure (say, a few hours at the all-you-can-eat buffet). This may be a quibble of interest only to philosophers, but there is a point of direct concern for us: that pleasure may well be the basis of happiness, but never in an extreme way, and never when divorced from our sense of what a good and purposeful life means.

2

Pleasure is Good
(The Epicureans)

Plato had been dead for seven years when Epicurus (341–271 BC) was born in an Athenian colony on the island of Samos in the Aegean Sea. The son of a schoolmaster, he became interested in philosophy as an adolescent. He first journeyed to Athens in 323 BC to begin his military service. Upon its completion he rejoined his family, by then relocated to Colophon in Asia Minor after the conquering Macedonians had expelled the Athenian colonists from Samos. For the next decade Epicurus continued to study philosophy. In 311 BC, aged thirty, he began teaching in Mytilene, and left soon afterwards for Lampsacus. Five years later he returned to Athens, where he taught for the remaining thirty-five years of his life.

Epicurus preached his radical philosophy at a time when Athens's grand democratic ideals had been jeopardised by despotism and civic unrest. Popular religion inspired not faith but bewilderment and terror. Plato and Aristotle, the great philosophers of the century that had just passed, no longer seemed relevant. In that troubling moment, succumbing to scepticism and despair seemed the easy way out. For anyone disenchanted with the way of the world yet still committed to leading the good life, the highly self-sufficient philosophy of Epicurus – to be happy, just seek pleasure – must have been powerfully seductive.

At no time was the seduction more effective than at the end of

Epicurus' own life. Unlike Socrates, Epicurus died of natural causes (kidney failure); but like his philosophical forebear, he drew his last breath surrounded by friends and followers. After climbing into a bronze tub filled with hot water, Epicurus drank a glass of wine, instructed his pupils to remember his teachings, and then peacefully drifted into unconsciousness. In the weeks prior to his death he had suffered agonising pain from kidney stones. Yet he insisted that he would die a blessed and happy man because his thoughts remained fixed on the joyful memory of conversations with friends. The over-powering pleasure that Epicurus derived from these memories, so he claimed, rendered him insensitive to pain. Cicero, writing two hundred years later, dismissed this as mere fustian: no memory, however ecstatic, can prevent anyone from feeling pain. A man exposed to unbearable heat does not comfort himself by remembering that he once took a cool bath.

We can never know whether Epicurus exaggerated on his deathbed. But we *do* know that with his dying words he imparted what he believed was the secret of happiness: storing up pleasure against rainy days of pain.

Philosophy (and other things) in a garden

Disaffected Athenians found themselves drawn to Epicurus because of his freethinking view that *everyone* could benefit from philosophy. 'Let no one,' he exhorted, 'delay the study of philosophy while young nor weary of it when old. For no one is either too young or too old for the health of the soul.'[1] Epicureans regarded philosophy as something of a team sport, and so they did it in groups; indeed, many of them lived in communes modelled on the one just outside Athens – called 'The Garden' – that the philosopher himself had established.

Within this secret garden lived both men and women, both free and slave. That servants and women enjoyed the same status as freemen made these communities socially reformist. But not collec-tivist: everyone retained private possessions since Epicurus believed that holding property in common implied that the members of the community mistrusted each other. Still, income was redistributed since the wealthier residents were expected to help finance the enterprise, which included copying and publishing Epicurean handbooks.

Partly because the community dared to include women (including those shady dames 'Baby Lion', 'Little Conquest' and 'Tits') and partly because it was cut off from the Athenian city-state, outsiders grew suspicious of this philosophical cult and its charismatic founder. Epicurus stood accused of perpetrating the very vices that he condemned. Timocrates, a disgruntled former student, claimed that Epicurus vomited twice a day because he consumed so many extravagant foods. The Stoic philosopher Epictetus, who lived three centuries later, continued the assault by branding Epicurus a 'foul-mouthed bastard'. More damningly, it was rumoured that orgies were held in the garden. The slanderous charges gained such credibility that Diogenes Laertius, writing some six hundred years after the fact, repeated them in his *Lives and Sayings of Famous Philosophers*. Much like a modern tabloid journalist, Diogenes started with the sensational aspect of the story: rumours of sexual depravity and accusations of indecent conduct. Only later, after his readers had been sufficiently titillated, did he bother to admit that the lurid allegations made against Epicurus were, in fact, false, and that the philosopher's moral character remained beyond reproach.

Tokens of thought

In the ancient world, you would have encountered philosophy in the shape of proverbs and (if you were among the few who could read) open letters. Once memorised, a proverb could be called to mind in an anxious moment. Letters gained a wide readership because they were passed from hand to hand. If you required a reassuringly material form of wisdom, you might inscribe a helpful proverb on to a picture frame or a favourite piece of jewellery. Sometimes words were unnecessary. A statue of Epicurus, his portrait or even his likeness carved on a signet ring: all could inspire deep thoughts in a believer. Far from being devoid of meaning, such objects served as tangible and encouraging reminders that wisdom lies within everyone's reach. For his more ambitious followers, Epicurus composed letters outlining the basic principles of his beliefs. These letters were not private correspondence but public documents; they were shared, copied and circulated, much like the letters of St Paul to the early Christians. And for the philosophical diehards willing to undertake intensive study, Epicurus wrote out his arguments in lengthy treatises.

Ranging from the simple to the complex, these varied forms of philosophical knowledge demanded of their users correspondingly varied levels of intellectual effort. But no one should sneer at the low end products hawked in the intellectual marketplace of the classical world, nor be driven by status anxiety to covet the high end ones. The crucial thing was not that everyone should progress from the easy to the difficult – from wearing lucky charms to reading lengthy treatises – but that everyone should find their own level. Whether carved in marble, set in gold or written on papyrus, philosophical knowledge was a valuable commodity never in short supply. The many and diverse tokens of Epicurean thought that circulated in the ancient world made the philosophical life available to anyone who wanted it, and in a way that made sense to them. For who wants a way of thinking about life that does not make sense?

Appropriately for someone who believed that ideas matter to all, Epicurus was a staggeringly prolific writer of philosophical and scientific treatises. His greatest work, *On Nature*, filled thirtyseven volumes (scrolls, actually; the book had yet to be invented), of which all that remain are papyrus fragments excavated at Herculaneum, the Roman town destroyed along with Pompeii when Mount Vesuvius erupted in AD 79. Discovered only in 1928, the fragments of this monumental work rested undisturbed for nearly nineteen hundred years. Of other works we know only the titles: *On Love*, *On Religion*, *On Fate* and *On Music*.

The only works of Epicurus that have been preserved in their entirety are three letters: the Letter to Herodotus is the simplified account of his philosophy written for beginning students; the Letter to Pythocles, on astronomy and meteorology, was probably written not by Epicurus himself but by one of his followers; and the Letter to Menoeceus – to which we will soon return – sets out his views on happiness. Also surviving are two collections of short epigrammatic texts known as the 'Principal Doctrines' and the 'Vatican Sayings'. They consist of the proverbs that Epicureans once memorised and recited, and thus give us a good idea of what the man himself taught about happiness.

The four principles of happiness

When Epicurus wrote to his friend Menoeceus about happiness, he focused upon the core elements that would be present in the life of *any* happy person. It never entered his mind to offer Menoeceus (or anybody else) advice on what to do in this or that situation. (Unlike the ancients, we expect, rather lazily, that theories of happiness will provide instant solutions to the most intractable problems.)

Epicurus emphasised that being happy meant subscribing to four fundamental principles:

- the gods exist, but not in the way we suppose
- death is nothing to fear
- pleasure is the key to happiness
- everything we need to be happy is easy to obtain

A happy person, says Epicurus, is someone who has correct beliefs about the gods, faces death without fear, pursues pleasure (but, as we shall see, in a highly qualified way) and recognises the value of prudence and simplicity. If we live by these values we will act wisely – so that we move closer to happiness; if not, then we will act unwisely – and thus cause ourselves to be unhappy. In either case, our actions are undertaken not in accordance with pre-existing rules or commandments ('thou shalt', 'thou shalt not') but in accordance with our own appraisal of the quality of our life as a whole.

The gods exist, but not in the way we suppose

Despite claims to the contrary made by his detractors, Epicurus taught that divine beings do exist and that we can possess clear knowledge of them. Yet he also taught that many of us hold false beliefs about the nature of the gods. Our mistake is to attribute to them traits that actually diminish or distort their perfection. We believe, for example, that the gods watch over us, take an interest in our affairs, reward us when we worship them, and punish us when we neglect them. In short, we believe that the gods behave just like us. Wrong, says Epicurus: the gods do not behave just like us, for the simple yet frequently ignored reason that they are *not* just like us.

The gods exist in a state of perpetual bliss (that is part of what makes them gods), and so remain untroubled by all that transpires in the world beneath them. 'Nothing cankers their peace of mind,' as the tormented Lucretius enviously observed.[2] (According to legend, the Roman poet killed himself after being driven mad by a love potion that his neglected wife, Lucilla, had slipped into his drink.) Since deities need nothing to fulfil their desires, they have no cause to intervene in our lives; in fact, they bear no responsibility for creating our planet and sustaining the life forms – including us – that inhabit it. In Epicurean cosmology the earth exists only as the accidental result of atoms colliding into each other as they move randomly throughout the universe.

Today, we are bound to find this a rather godless view of God: if he didn't create the world and if he doesn't love us, then why bother worshipping him? Why, indeed, Epicurus would reply. Happiness begins, he would go on to say, with the realisation – initially unnerving, but then liberating – that the gods do not condescend to involve themselves in our affairs. To believe otherwise is to deny ourselves any chance of happiness. For when we worry that the gods are going to punish us we succeed only in making ourselves miserable. And you don't have to be an ancient Greek to believe, as many people do, that mankind's freedom is a freedom from the superstitious fear of God.

Death is nothing to fear

Though widespread, the fear of death is irrational and absurd. To fear something, such as disease or imprisonment, means that we think its consequences are bad; to desire something, such as health or freedom, means we think its consequences are good. Yet to know whether something is good or bad, Epicurus believes, we must first experience it, directly or vicariously. (Children know that it is bad to touch a hot stove only after burning their fingers doing it.) Death, however, is something that we can never experience because it is nothing other than the *end* of experience. We will all undergo the experience of dying, as Epicurus acknowledges; but that is not the same as being dead. Nor can we contact the departed to find out what being dead is like. Thus, we can never be in a legitimate position to call death good or bad. And if we cannot call death bad then we cannot rationally fear it. 'Death is nothing to us,' Epicurus taught. 'When we exist, death is not yet present, and when death is present, then we do not exist.'³ For both the quick and the dead, death is irrelevant.

Moreover, the fear of death is absurd, because it leads us to feel pain about something that has not yet happened – and something that may not be painful when it does happen. Only a fool, Epicurus contends, would fear the *prospect* of death. Those who fear death because they believe the gods will punish them in the afterlife spend this life frightened that they will suffer the everlasting torments of hell. Others fear death because they are convinced there is no afterlife. Saddened by the possibility of oblivion, they mourn their own deaths prematurely. All this worry and anxiety causes a great deal of harm, Epicurus believed, by distracting us from the very things that are necessary for our happiness. We traumatise ourselves with the threat of eternal damnation and depress ourselves with the thought that we do not possess an immortal soul. All too easily, death casts a pall over life.

Epicurus is telling us that in this world we are fundamentally free. He says that there are no gods who once created us, now watch over us and will punish us either in this life or the next. Indeed, there is no afterlife, at least not one that we can experience in any immediate way. Released from the bondage of superstition, whether a mistaken belief about the gods or an irrational fear of death, we find that happiness is possible in our earthly state of perfect freedom. Instead of worrying about punishment in the next world, we should focus on eliminating the anxiety we feel in *this* world. That way, happiness lies.

Pleasure is the key to happiness

We seek pleasure, but we may not do just as we please. Not because there is an absolute moral framework for judging actions (no such thing exists, says Epicurus) but because we realise that some actions will increase our happiness and others diminish it. For Epicurus, the correct standard for judging our actions is not whether they conform to a moral code, but whether they make us feel tranquil – that is, free from anxiety. There is no other way to measure the rightness (or wrongness) of our actions. Our rational self-interest tells us that we should perform an action if it will make us tranquil and refrain if it will make us anxious. In this way, reason and pleasure walk hand-in-hand. (Nowadays, we are likely to think of reason and pleasure as opposites: the mind's controlling force declares war on the body's uncontrollable passions.)

How can we know with certainty whether a particular action leads to tranquillity or anxiety? If we can't be certain, then we have no option but to act randomly, learn from hard experience and hope for the best result. That is a dangerously inefficient way to live, for there is no guarantee that we would make the right decision. We must be certain. Epicurus anticipated as much, for he declared that we *can* know which actions will (or won't) promote our happiness – once we learn to distinguish between necessary and unnecessary desires. We will be able to identify those desires that deserve to be satisfied, those that should be deferred and those that must be renounced.

Our deliberations will not be overly complex, Epicurus predicted, because there are only three kinds of desires: natural and necessary (those that liberate us from pain); natural but unnecessary (those that liberate us from pain, but may cause harm); and unnatural and unnecessary (those that do not liberate us from pain and may cause harm). No desire can be unnatural *and* necessary since those terms are mutually exclusive. We embrace a desire to the extent that it leads towards the tranquillity in which happiness consists, and we resist it to the extent that it leads away from tranquillity. Thus, we *must* satisfy desires that are natural and necessary because they are vital to our happiness. We *may* satisfy desires that are natural but unnecessary, as long as they cause us no harm. And we *should never* satisfy desires that are unnatural and unnecessary because they are not conducive to happiness.

Everything we need to be happy is easy to obtain

It is easy to obtain all things necessary for our happiness and difficult to obtain all things unnecessary for it. Luxurious versions of basic things – Prada shoes, a Bentley, a villa in Tuscany – require time and money not just to acquire but also to maintain. We enjoy such luxuries (who wouldn't?), but we must not, Epicurus warned, become dependent upon them. Being greedy – wanting more than we need – will only reduce our chance of happiness. If we crave luxuries then it will become harder and harder to be satisfied. No shoes will be stylish enough, no car fast enough, no house palatial enough.

Our own experience tells us this all the time: that the pleasure we derive from any object gradually declines as we get used to it. The charming scientific name for this process is 'hedonic adaptation': the moment we get used to something nice, it stops feeling nice. Buying a new car is the classic example of becoming habituated to an object of desire. At first, your expensive Jaguar gives you a great deal of enjoyment. But sooner or later, it won't seem any more attractive than the less expensive Volvo that it replaced. And so you start fantasising about your next car, in an unstoppable, but forlorn, hope that it will be the one to completely satisfy your desire. Of course it won't – because in the chain of desire, there is no last link. Many of us today are trapped in a spiral of consumption that compels us to buy ever more extravagant items to maintain a consistent amount of pleasure. At some point, and it arrives sooner and sooner, pleasure turns first to boredom, then to dissatisfaction and, finally, to anxiety. We torture ourselves by asking why our hard-earned possessions fail to make us happy. The persistence of unsatisfied desire is a theme that arises in many philosophies of happiness, both Eastern and Western. It is a truth universally acknowledged that luxuries can never make us truly content because they satisfy our desires only temporarily.

So the secret of happiness is to attain the state of tranquillity in which we no longer need to satisfy any desire, no longer need to pursue any pleasure. This is a secret easily unravelled. We seek pleasure only when we are in pain. If we are no longer in pain (for that is what it means to be tranquil), then we will no longer seek pleasure. Thus, we make decisions about desire – indulge this one, defer that one, suppress yet another – not in terms of the desire itself, but in terms of what is good for our life as a whole.

This broader perspective stops us from being profligate in our quest for pleasure. In a sober frame of mind, we will think clearly and carefully about how best to reduce the turmoil in our souls. We will find that simple things yield as much pleasure as luxuries. And once we grow accustomed to simple things we will have a better time in life because we will appreciate luxuries all the more when, or if, they come along. 'Those who least need extravagance enjoy it most', was Epicurus' home truth.[4]

All of the pleasure, none of the guilt

Many of us will find it puzzling that Epicurus unites pleasure and virtue, especially if our heritage is Judaeo-Christian or Islamic, since we might well have been taught that pleasure and virtue exist in inverse proportion: the more pleasure we feel, the less virtuous we become. Hence, the phrase 'guilty pleasures'. Such an expression would have been meaningless to Epicurus, who found nothing illicit in the desire for pleasure. Among his contemporaries, the Stoics (of whom Seneca was a later example) believed that pleasure and virtue were *separate* things because the wicked and the unhappy do enjoy pleasure.

But for Epicureans pleasure is the *sole* motive for action because it is the only standard for judging the rightness of conduct. An act is moral if it produces more pleasure than pain; immoral if it produces more pain than pleasure. So when making ethical judgements, we should consider neither the action itself (is it right to do *x*?) nor its consequences for others (if I do *x*, what will happen?) but only the *emotions* that it will arouse within us (if I do *x*, will it make me feel good?). Plainly this is a relative, not an absolute, standard. The same act, when performed by different people, or by the same person but under different circumstances, can be both moral (if it brings pleasure) and immoral (if it brings pain).

Within this closed system, virtue – the disposition to act morally – is not an end in itself but a means to pleasure. We are virtuous not because we like virtue (or at least not necessarily) but because we like the pleasure that comes from it. It is impossible, then, for an Epicurean to imagine a virtue that does not automatically entail pleasure. Virtue will not reside in one fixed place because, under the right circumstances, many different actions can be virtuous. Yet wherever virtue is found, pleasure will also be there. And happiness, too.

Cicero, in his dialogue *On the Ends of Goods and Evils*, provides an instructive example of how virtue and pleasure always turn up together. The virtuous man will be courageous, Cicero explains, not because he esteems courage but because he desires to live without anxiety. And exhibiting courage is a highly effective way to have an anxiety-free life. Similarly, the virtuous man is temperate not because he values temperance, but because he values the peace of mind that it begets. For the ancient Greeks and Romans, temperance was a broad character trait: the strength to act moderately in all types of situations. It meant far more than our narrow modern sense of merely abstaining from alcohol.

Still, we can use the familiar scenario of knowing your limit at the pub. Let's say that you prefer not to be hung over on Sunday morning, and so you make sure that you don't get drunk on Saturday night. Epicurus would say that makes you virtuous (you stay in command of your faculties, which is the virtue of temperance) and therefore happy. But remember: you acted that way not in order to be virtuous but in order to have pleasure (in this case, the pleasure of not facing a hangover). Yet in obtaining that pleasure you found that you were also being virtuous. You found that you were happy.

It hurts so good

A happy life is not simply one in which at any moment pleasure outweighs pain. All pleasures are good, but not all should be pursued; all pains are bad, but not all should be avoided. As Epicurus taught, we must choose our pleasures and pains judiciously. It is wisdom to understand that sometimes we reject pleasure and accept pain in order to secure a greater, more lasting pleasure.

By stopping himself from getting drunk, the temperate man wins for himself a higher pleasure – tranquillity – by renouncing a lower one. The intemperate man, however, eagerly obtains his modest pleasures (which, as Cicero tartly observes, are unconnected with true happiness), but then he also suffers vastly disproportionate pains: disease, poverty, disgrace and, finally, imprisonment. Cicero is using an extreme example to make the general point that the single-minded pursuit of pleasure is not always our best course of action.

We make pleasure–pain calculations every single day. Not all of them are high-minded. Many people pay to do something in their leisure time that they probably avoid doing at school, at home or in the office: raising and lowering heavy objects. Although painful and boring, 'working out' does yield pleasurable results: greater strength, increased energy and a dramatically improved ability to attract sexual partners. Surely all these long-term pleasures are worth a little short-term pain. (There's a chain of fitness clubs in Washington, DC, called Results, an establishment whose very name exhorts its body-conscious clientele to discount immediate pains and focus on promised glories.) If you have ever invoked the mantra 'no pain, no gain' beloved of fitness freaks everywhere, then Epicurus would be proud of you (after all, the ancient Greeks invented gym culture); but he would also think that you could find better things to do with your time than building up your biceps.

Sometimes, it's best to renounce pleasure. An increasing number of American teenagers from families on the religious right have publicly sworn to abstain from pre-marital sex because they believe – to quote *their* mantra – that 'true love waits'. A recent television documentary featured 'Texas Teenage Virgins' taking just this kind of 'purity pledge'. (Yet as the staff of the local STD clinic revealed, some of these 'technical' virgins had no qualms about engaging in oral and anal sex. God, it seems, cares only about vaginal penetration.)

Epicurus would have mixed feelings about voluntary abstinence, however creatively defined. He would reject outright the religious motive – on the grounds that there is no god who dictates moral standards – but would admire the restraint. But the larger point he would make to the purity pledge-takers is that wise people behave prudently, not recklessly. They forsake pleasure and endure pain *only* when those sacrifices enable them to enjoy greater pleasure or to avoid greater pain. In itself, the sacrifice is meaningless. So if, like Texas teenage virgins, you're going to renounce pleasure, then you'd better have a compelling reason; otherwise, there's no point. You're just being false to your own nature.

No matter how much pain we suffer, our pleasure – if it is of the highest sort – remains undiminished. And if our pleasure is undiminished, then so, too, is our happiness. It was for this reason – the highest pleasures are indestructible – that Epicurus claimed that a wise person would remain happy even while being tortured. (The type of person Epicurus had in mind was an innocent victim, not someone who deserved punishment.) This is a bizarre claim for anyone to make, but especially bizarre for someone who believes that pleasure is the font of happiness. Leaving aside sado-masochistic rituals practised by consenting adults, surely no pleasure can arise from torture. So how can it be possible that the wise man remains happy while pain is inflicted upon him?

No contradiction arises, Epicurus declares, for a reason that we have already seen. In all circumstances – and especially a circumstance like torture – the wise person focuses neither on the activity (in this case, torture) nor its consequences (in this case, pain), but on his *attitude* towards the activity (its inability to overpower his happiness). Once a person is already happy then neither accident nor misfortune, neither calamity nor injury, can diminish his happiness. Since happiness is a pronouncement upon one's life as a whole – and thus detached from any particular episode or experience – it cannot be dislodged by a single moment of suffering. On this point, the Epicureans and the Stoics agree.

Because the proper pursuit of pleasure is not about thrill seeking, not about living for the moment, our ultimate goal cannot be to experience as many different pleasures as possible. Rather, it must be to achieve the state of tranquillity in which we feel no pain. Indeed, the greatest pleasure, insists Epicurus, arises from the complete absence of pain. When I experience the lack of any desire that needs to be fulfilled I find myself in a state of pleasurable tranquillity; nothing convulses me, nothing disquiets me.

Such pleasures will vary in kind (because they will have different causes) but never in degree, for there is a totality to the absence of pain that cannot be qualified. When pain is absent it is fully so, and the resulting pleasure is similarly full because nothing stands in its way. The highest pleasures are perfect and, like perfection, they can be neither measured nor quantified. It is impossible for these pleasures to be made more intense because they already exist – only ever *can* exist – in their maximum intensity. Thus, while Epicurus speaks of attaining happiness he does not speak (like Bentham) of maximising it, as if someone could acquire *more* happiness by behaving differ-ently. To attain true happiness means that you've already, as they say, 'maxed out'.

This makes for a nice theory, but does it work in practice? Does anyone actually experience pleasure in the absence of pain? Imagine a man, tired and thirsty, wandering in the desert. On the point of collapse, he finally reaches an oasis with cool, clear water. What will give him the most pleasure? A drink of water, naturally. Not so, says Epicurus. The thirsty man's greatest pleasure lies not in having his thirst quenched but in no longer being thirsty. What our dehydrated wanderer really desires, according to Epicurus, is not the pleasure of drinking but the absence of the pain – parched throat and cracked, blistered lips – that makes him want to drink in the first place. The happy man is not he who drinks when thirsty but he who has no thirst. It's not that we want food, drink and shelter (although that's how we experience it) but that we want *not* to be hungry, *not* to be thirsty, *not* to be cold. We become truly happy not when we satisfy our desires but in the *next* moment – the moment when we realise that we have no desires left.

Accentuate the negative

Our intuitive understanding of pleasure – *feeling good* – is not one that Epicurus fully shares. Otherwise, he would not say things like 'not being thirsty is a great pleasure'. The difference between Epicurus and us is that he believes in two distinct kinds of pleasure: positive and negative.

Positive pleasure depends on pain because it is nothing other than the *removal* of pain – you're thirsty, so you drink a glass of water. Negative pleasure, however, is the state of equilibrium in which you no longer feel pain and thus no longer need any (positive) pleasure to get rid of that pain – you're not thirsty, so you don't need to drink a glass of water. Positive pleasures are *kinetic* because they imply activity: eating, drinking, listening to music, having sex. Such pleasures seem actual or real because they entail direct sensory experience. In drinking a glass of water when thirsty I am actually doing something; moreover, I am doing something quantifiable: I can drink a little or a lot.

Negative pleasures, by contrast, are *static* because they imply inactivity: *not* eating because I am full, *not* drinking because my thirst is already quenched, *not* listening to music because I have heard enough, *not* having sex because I am not aroused. Such pleasures seem nebulous because they do not entail direct sensory experience. Precisely because they arise from the lack of pain, they entail only indirect experience – that is, the pleasurable state of having no unfulfilled desires. This type of pleasure cannot be quantified, cannot be understood in terms of more and less. 'How much are you not hungry?' is a nonsensical question.

Epicurus upholds the superiority of negative pleasures because he believes them to be total and complete. To be truly happy we should seek not the limited kinetic pleasure that comes from satisfying a particular desire but the boundless static pleasure – the absence of pain – that comes from having no desires that need satisfying in the first place. When every desire is fulfilled then every pain will vanish and we will reach the very limit of all possible pleasure. Epicurus promises that in happiness we will rival Zeus himself. Positive pleasures we must regard as inferior because they are necessarily partial and incomplete: our clothes could always be more stylish, our meals more savoury, our orgasms more volcanic. As long as we have such unfulfilled desires we will be in pain. In happiness, we will lag far behind Zeus.

Once we understand that Epicurus defined the highest pleasure negatively – the absence of pain – we can see how unfairly he has been judged, not just by his contemporaries but by posterity. Despite centuries of rumours to the contrary, Epicurus was no soft voluptuary. That much we know from his letter to Menoeceus:

> When, therefore, we say that pleasure is the end, we do not mean the pleasures of the dissolute and those [pleasures] that lie in enjoyment, as some suppose who are ignorant and disagree with us or take it in a bad sense, but rather not being pained in body and not being troubled in soul.[5]

Whenever we call someone with a taste for fine wines and gourmet food an 'epicure', we abuse the term. In truth, such people are degenerate epicures because they seek only to maximise positive pleasures. The genuine epicure, who prizes only negative pleasures, leads a spartan and ascetic existence. The strict logic of Epicurean ethics allows for nothing else: we are happy only when tranquil; we are tranquil only when free from pain; we are free from pain only when all desires are fulfilled; desires can be fulfilled only if they are moderate.

Correctly understood, Epicureanism is never a licence for over-indulgence but always a pledge of austerity. Its ethical principles demand discipline and discernment. 'How serious, how temperate, how austere,' Cicero approvingly observed, 'is the school that is supposed to be sensual, lax and luxurious.'[6] You will not lead a life worthy of happiness if you are wanton and licentious. Indeed, it is precisely the harsh side of Epicurean philosophy that explains why early Christian theologians recognised the merit of its strict ethics, even if they could not countenance its disavowal of God's presence in history. In truth, being an epicure doesn't sound much like fun.

Epicurus maintains that the temperate man is happy because he has avoided the pains suffered by the intemperate man. For example, he takes pleasure in his sobriety, knowing that he is not hung over. But does that ring true? Can the mere absence of something, even something as distasteful as a hangover, be called a pleasure? It can barely be called an experience. The pleasure of waking up sober is a phantom pleasure. You can't really grasp it; and even if you could, it's far too bland to be enjoyable. You'd have to be a very particular kind of person – a recovering alcoholic, say – to feel that waking up sober is a great pleasure. And being a recovering alcoholic is a traumatically high price to pay for the pleasure of sobriety. Surely, if anybody is enjoying pleasure it's the *intemperate* man, for his pleasures are palpable: he can see, smell and taste his whisky. True, if he drinks too deeply from the cup of pleasure he may repent the morning after; but the morning's pain cannot erase the pleasures of the night before.

Still, Epicurus insists that negative pleasures are the only ones worth having. And yet the nagging problem is that negative pleasures don't look like pleasures, at least not the kind of pleasures that we're accustomed to having. If you think that Epicurus is inconsistent in how he defines pleasure, then you are thinking just like Cicero. He accused the Greek philosopher of intellectual sleight of hand, trying to make us believe that two different things – pleasure and pain – are one and the same.

Sneering at the masses

Cicero was no knee-jerk critic. As a youth he attended lectures given by the Epicurean teacher Phaedrus. In the *Tusculan Disputations* he betrayed more sympathy for the Stoics, but he did give the Epicureans a fair shake. Ultimately, he rejected the philosophy of Epicurus because it relied too heavily upon sensory data, exalted pleasure, precluded any possibility of divine intervention and, most worryingly of all for the great Roman statesman, it devalued public life. Cicero was convinced that anyone who practised Epicurean teachings risked leading a life of sheer indolence, perhaps even debauchery. Anyone who, like Cicero, was committed to life in the civic arena would find little to satisfy them in Epicurus' renouncing spirit.

Cicero's reasons for doubting the Epicurean vision of happiness are his reasons, not ours. Many of us would not, for example, demand that happiness be open to the possibility of divine intervention. But one of Cicero's concerns we probably *do* share: the expectation that a happy life is connected to the world, not divorced from it. Part of being happy means that we are at home in the world as we find it.

But inside the walled garden on the outskirts of Athens, the pupils of Epicurus learned a different lesson: that the good life meant being cut off from the business – and busyness – of the world outside. To desire what the world desires was to make the prospect of happiness even more remote. The values of public life – fame, respect, status and wealth – were no values at all, and such insubstantial pleasures quickly faded. Worse, the statesman ran the risk of slander and defeat, and his reputation was never secure. Such a life was too fragile a basis for happiness. We would be much better off, Epicurus counselled, with a life of quiet contentment. And so the only option, if we truly wanted to achieve the state of tranquillity necessary for happiness, was to withdraw from the world and limit our community to a few like-minded friends. That is why Epicurus, true to his beliefs, chose the secret garden over the public square.

Inspired by his founding example, the followers of Epicurus, for many centuries, sought refuge on a metaphorical mountaintop where they aspired to lives of serenity and tranquillity. From the purified heights they looked down with satisfaction (and occasional smugness) upon the confused mass of humanity who lacked the wisdom to choose rightly between pleasure and pain. Their 'greatest joy', Lucretius declared, was

> to stand aloof in a quiet citadel, stoutly fortified by the teaching of the wise, and to gaze down from that elevation on others wandering aimlessly in a vain search for the way of life, pitting their wits one against another, disputing for preference, struggling night and day with unstinted effort to scale the pinnacles of wealth and power. O joyless hearts of men! O minds without vision![7]

It is not difficult to see why Epicureanism has been criticised as a socially immature model for happiness. Since it flourishes most fully in separatist groups it can become something of a cult; and by placing so much emphasis on individual self-sufficiency it can become isolating. After all, Epicureans are concerned only with how they feel. How *other* people feel does not directly concern them. True, they value justice and friendship – but only to the extent that such things affect their own lives. Whatever touches them not, concerns them not. Epicureans might care little for luxuries, but they care enormously about themselves.

Part II
Conquering Desire

3

Get Busy with Your Works (Hinduism)

To know the secret of the universe you must drink a glass of salt water. That is the teaching of the *Chandogya Upanishad*, one of the most ancient Hindu scriptures, dating back several thousand years. (*Upanishad* translates as 'sit down near', which tells us that they were originally composed as stories to be listened to, not read.) The tale is a simple one: after spending twelve years studying sacred texts with a guru, Shvetaketu returns home to his father, Uddalaka Aruni. Proudly, he declares that he knows everything that can be known. His father is a bit sceptical of this claim, but not for the reason we might suppose. We might suppose that no one could possibly know everything, even if a lifetime were spent reading books. Uddalaka Aruni believed that we *could* know everything – even the innermost secret of the universe – but books were not the way to find it.

Taking a more practical approach, he devises an experiment to teach his son the true nature of reality. He tells Shvetaketu to place a chunk of salt in a jug of water, leave it overnight and then return with it the next morning. The following day Shvetaketu arrives with the jug of water. His father asks him to remove the chunk of salt. So he plunges his hand into the water and searches for the salt. Nothing. It dissolved overnight. His father now asks Shvetaketu to sip from one side of the jug:

'How does the water taste?' he asks.

'Salty.'

'Now sip from the middle. How does it taste?'

'Salty.'

'Now sip from the other side. How does it taste?'

'Salty.'[1]

This is the secret of the universe: every drop of water tastes salty. Or, rather, this is the metaphor through which the secret is revealed. The salt water, as Uddalaka Aruni explains, symbolises the universe – or ultimate reality, or the hidden nature of things as they truly are. Just as every drop of salt water contains salt, every part of the universe contains its own essence. Among the many parts of the universe are individual selves like you and me. So within you and me lies the essence of ultimate reality. Of course we cannot see it, but we can trust that it is there within us – like a grain of salt dissolved in water.

Baffling though it appears from a Western perspective, the existence of absolute reality within each person is Hinduism's most fundamental truth, and the basis of its teachings about happiness. As Shvetaketu's father realised, this truth cannot be acquired through mere book learning, but must be experienced directly. Hence, the salt water experiment – which conveys instantly a truth that Shvetaketu never found in all the weighty tomes that he had studied so carefully. This truth, far from being distant and remote, is something we experience all the time, even if we cannot express it as philosophers and theologians. Yet we do not need to do so, for we may trust our instincts and our feelings.

Whenever we hunger for something, whenever we feel that we have not lived up to our potential, we are feeling nothing other than the presence within us of absolute reality. If we did not intuit a higher reality, then how else could we know we were not measuring up to it? As the Hindu mystic Ramakrishna (1836–86) understood, we typically experience the absolute as a gap to be filled, a yearning to be satisfied or a bridge to be crossed:

> Man is always restless, always moving from place to place … [The] fact that he is dissatisfied with his finite nature shows that it is not his natural condition. The fact that he has infinite ambition, that he has insatiable hunger for more and more, proves that he is infinite by nature …[2]

Unsettling as Ramakrishna's words are, they are consoling, too, for we can take comfort in knowing that a feeling of discontent – the question that comes relentlessly from inside our head, *what if?* – is the blessed reminder that we are 'infinite by nature'. What first appear to be testaments to failure are, if we look more closely, signs of a greater reality that, at least for now, we only imperfectly understand, only clumsily grasp. The finite and dissatisfied self we carry around day after day (like an extra suitcase we wished we had not packed) is not our true self; our true self is infinite. This means that although the universe transcends us, it also includes us.

The effort to understand such a truth is the path to happiness – or salvation, or liberation, or enlightenment, which are different names in Hinduism for the same thing. So, in this chapter, when we look at how Hindus search for enlightenment, or meditate upon absolute reality, or manifest their love of a favoured deity, we are looking at the multiple dimensions of the search for happiness.

But whatever form it takes, the search for happiness in the Hindu tradition begins with the intuitive knowledge that the individual and the cosmic are identical; that the essence of one's true self and the essence of absolute reality can no more be separated than salt from salt water. This knowledge can transform our lives by ushering in new habits of thought, action and feeling which help us to become the greater, more developed self to which we aspire; the self that, through the power of karma, wins release from the eternal cycle of birth, death and rebirth.

The Bhagavad Gita

Someone who struggled to become a better version of himself was Prince Arjuna, the hero of the *Bhagavad Gita* (*c.* 300 BC), the devotional poem whose popularity and authority in Hindu culture have remained unsurpassed for more than two millennia. The *Gita* – 'The Lord's Song' – is a poetic reflection on the duty and destiny of mankind. No aspect of human life falls outside this staggeringly audacious work.

The story opens on a battlefield, where the Kauravas are fighting their cousins, the Pandavas. (The great Hindu epic the *Mahabharata*, of which the *Gita* forms just one part, tells the full story of this conflict.) Prince Arjuna, a young Pandava warrior, refuses to fight his cousins. Krishna, his warlord companion – but actually the god Vishnu in human guise – entreats him to join the battle. Their conversation makes up almost the entire poem. After explaining to Arjuna why he should take up arms, Krishna sets out a grand view of human life, which forms the climax of the *Gita*. What appears to be a rousing battle cry becomes an awe-inspiring revelation of the universe's hidden structure and secret purpose.

Meanwhile, the rival clans, their weapons drawn, stand ready to attack each other. As a war story, the *Gita* is absurd: combat is suspended while on the sidelines two soldiers contemplate the nature of the universe. But that is just the point; the absurdity of the plot tells us that plot is not integral to the story's larger meaning. The interrupted battle is but the occasion, the excuse, for the main event – which is Krishna teaching Arjuna about the nature of reality.

Throughout the poem, Arjuna stands in, as it were, for us, because we, too, are searching for the key to the answer to life's great questions. (We shall come back to Arjuna soon, for he serves as a model for the different ways of creating happiness in our lives.) To the great and mysterious question 'how do we find happiness?', the *Gita* offers three answers: through the way of knowledge, the way of action and the way of love. In truth, this is but one answer, for all three paths to happiness are manifestations of the same disciplined approach to forging a link, or closing the gap, between the self and absolute reality. This discipline goes by a name that is familiar, yet frequently misunderstood: yoga.

Yoga: *path to happiness*

An old Indian story tells of Viveka, a newborn prince, whose enemies in the royal household put him into a basket and sent it floating down the river. The infant was rescued from death by a peasant couple who raised him as their own. (This is the story of Moses, but with the social classes reversed.) Unaware of his true birth, Viveka suspected that he had come from somewhere else, because his true mother, his true family and his true home all appeared to him in dreams. On his sixteenth birthday he left in search of them. After journeying for more than seven years, he found his way back to his true home. When he reached the royal palace, where his family had waited so long for his return, he discovered that the king, his real father, had died. Viveka knew that *he* was now king, yet struggled to find his kingly nature; raised in a world of poverty and hardship, he knew only how to be a peasant. Over time, and under the patient guidance of teachers, Viveka cast off his comfortable yet mistaken identity and embraced the strange new reality of the person that, unbeknownst to himself, he had been all along.

Of course Viveka is not a real person, and there never was a peasant who, by some outrageous good fortune, turned out to be a prince. Viveka cannot be real because he is something more than real: he is an archetype, a revealing pattern for the course of human life. In this pattern of separation and reunion we might recognise that we ourselves feel divorced from our true nature and long to be reunited with it. Viveka's mythical search through the jungles of north India is the symbol of our actual search for the true but hidden self; hidden, yet waiting for us to find it; waiting for us to come home.

This reunion with the self, this homecoming, is achieved through yoga, the discipline that enables us to surrender our mistaken identity and recover our true one. Such a definition will appear strange to Westerners who have experienced yoga mostly as a fitness regime of contorted and painful poses held for long stretches of time. This is a caricature; but like all caricatures, it captures a truth. Some (though not all) forms of yoga, because they emphasise posture, movement and breath control, do indeed bring about a greater sense of physical well-being. Desirable such results may be, but they were not what the original yogins aimed to achieve. They sought a breakthrough in awareness, a heightened concentration of the mind – making it 'one-pointed' – on the nature of absolute, ultimate reality. Long before Freud and Jung invented modern psychoanalysis, the yogins of ancient India had begun to master the unconscious, controlling its wayward impulses and irrational desires. To reach that state of unified consciousness, the yogin probably will rely upon meditation and controlled breathing; but those techniques for disciplining and controlling the body are employed for the sake of the mind – to free it from distraction and desire.

Westerners who practise yoga as a form of exercise and relaxation do not always have this greater goal in mind. To understand this deeper meaning of yoga, a bit of etymology may help. Yoga derives from the Sanskrit root *yuj*, meaning 'to link', 'to yoke' or 'to unite'. Just what are the things to be linked? Nothing other than the individual self and absolute reality. Through yoga, the self awakens to its true identity, an identity that it discovers to be the same as the cosmos. (This is the same principle as the indivisibility of the salt and the salt water.) As one contemporary teacher has put it, yoga is a 'reunion' with the truth.

Although traditionally associated with Hinduism and Buddhism, yoga remains open to those of any faith or none. It invokes no particular deity, no formal set of religious beliefs. Neither Eastern nor Western, sacred nor profane, the path of yoga is universally human. Nor is there just one path. Over the centuries, different styles of yoga have developed in India, and among the most prominent are:

- the way of knowledge (*jnana yoga*)
- the way of duty (*karma yoga*)
- the way of love (*bhakti yoga*)

We can make sense of these different paths in two ways: locally and globally. In terms of India's unique caste structure, *jnana yoga* developed for the intellectual elite, *karma yoga* for high-caste Brahmins and *bhakti yoga* – the populist style – for everybody else. For our purposes, though, the global dimension is what really matters. We are interested, primarily, in what the Hindu tradition (or *any* tradition) has to say about our own search for happiness. What can we learn about happiness from this ancient culture that we could not learn somewhere else?

The first thing we learn is that the ingredients of happiness – knowledge, duty and loving devotion – contrast sharply with the belief so prevalent in the modern West that happiness lies in the satisfaction of physical and material desires. Duty and happiness seem to be a flat contradiction. We might avoid doing our duty (because it is unpleasant or tiresome); but never would we avoid being happy (because it is joyful and carefree, or at least that's the prevailing stereotype). But that is not how to look at things, at least not from the Hindu perspective. In that tradition, the practise of yoga tells us that happiness is not a condition of self-satisfaction but a dynamic directed *outward* – towards knowledge of something greater than yourself, duty to your community and loving devotion shown to others. Yoga does begin with the self, but its ultimate purpose is to transcend the self by connecting it to a more profound awareness of what is absolutely and eternally real.

Secondly, and perhaps more importantly, we learn that our path to happiness must be *our* path; it must be tailor-made, suited to our temperaments and talents. There is no point embarking upon the journey to happiness only to realise that you are taking the wrong (that is, somebody else's) route. Pressing the point, we could say that the three yogic paths align themselves, broadly speaking, with

three different social roles or personality types: the secluded intellectual (*jnana yoga*), the dutiful worker and citizen (*karma yoga*) and the
loving devotee (*bhakti yoga*). To be sure, these paths are not separate
and distinct but actually weave themselves around each other, like
strands in a rope that gain strength when pulled together.

What seems to me the highest value of all these paths is that they
are inclusive: *everybody*, no matter who they are, what they are like
or what they do, can find happiness in a way that is right for them.
What they reveal is that our path to happiness must begin on our
doorstep, where we live; otherwise it is not ours. We do not have to
forge a new life – the one we have will do just fine – nor must we wait
for a more opportune moment – the right moment is always now. To
be happy we must rub *with* the grain of our character, not against it;
we must become the perfected version of the person we already are,
not someone whom we could never be. Only then can we, like the
wandering Viveka, find our way back home.

The cloud of ignorance

Suppose you mistake a coiled rope on the floor for a snake. What you
perceive through your senses – a rope – is true (you are not halluci-
nating); but what you make of it – a snake – is false. Deluded about
the actual nature of what lies before you, you impose a wrong perception upon it. But there is more. So powerful is your delusion that it
begins to influence your actions. Believing the rope to be a snake, you
might run away from it, try to kill it, or just stand frozen and start
screaming. This illusory snake produces real effects. (If you doubt
that illusions produce real effects, try explaining to the police as they
really handcuff you that you were only pretending to rob the bank
with your toy gun.)

To run away from a coiled rope because you believe it to be a snake
is what it means to be trapped in a world of delusion: actions, because
they arise from ignorance, never fit the true state of affairs. Delusion is
to be avoided for many reasons, but chiefly because it prevents us from

being happy. And it was precisely to lift the cloud of ignorance, to dispel illusions and to foster true knowledge, that *jnana yoga* emerged in India more than a thousand years ago.

The philosopher Shankara (AD 788–820), the first great teacher of *jnana yoga*, asserted that happiness could be achieved through knowledge alone. (He meant this partly as Hinduism's challenge to Buddhism, then an upstart rival, which maintained that the secret of happiness was not perfect knowledge but controlled desire.) The knowledge that Shankara had in mind was not anything that could be learned from sense perception ('grass is green') or demonstrated through reason ('all points on a circle are equidistant from the centre'). Rather, he meant the most profound knowledge that anyone could possess: the knowledge that the individual self and absolute reality are identical.

Even in Shankara's day, and that was twelve hundred years ago, there was nothing new about this claim; in fact, it had been taught for centuries in the *Upanishads* (especially in the tale of Shvetaketu and the salt water). Shankara's innovation was to declare that knowledge alone was sufficient to make anyone happy. In other words, once you possess this knowledge you will become happy, and unless you possess it you will never be happy. Devotional acts, religious icons and other ritualised forms of worship might inspire the necessary knowledge, but could never substitute for it.

Unfortunately, this sort of knowledge is difficult to comprehend beyond a merely superficial level, as the gurus would admit. Worse, we prevent ourselves from acquiring it by stubbornly clinging to an illusion of the self. We keep on believing that the self (what makes me *me* and you *you*) is no more than some dominant aspect or attribute of a person. In ordinary conversation we often speak of people (including ourselves) as if their essence, their true nature, were confined to one obvious way in which we encounter them. Thus, we say 'he's all heart' or 'she lives in her head'. Even as we give licence to such caricatures we know that they mislead. We all have felt the frustration not just of being misunderstood, but of being unable to put across our true self. Thwarted, we lament that 'I wasn't myself tonight' or 'she doesn't see what's inside me'. Far too often, we have the lingering and disquieting sense that the person we really are, deep down, never comes into view.

What *is* this buried self that we struggle to bring to the surface? To put the question that way is to get it wrong. Wrong because the true self cannot be reduced to what we can experience of someone, whether their body, their feelings, their thoughts, their actions, or all of them put together. Such things are mere appearances, and in time will perish. The real self, authentic and imperishable, is the soul. Even if we learn that much from the Hindu scriptures – and it is a great deal to learn – we are still apt to mistake the soul for the 'I' that we experience in normal, everyday life. The 'I' that is born, grows old, dies and is reborn (again and again, in the karmic cycle) is a false illusory self – like the coiled rope mistaken for a snake. The true self is immortal and infinite. Until we can *experience* that absolute truth (which is something quite different from getting our heads around it) we can never find happiness, for happiness is nothing other than entering into that truth.

The story of Viveka, the peasant who discovers that he is a prince, dramatises this very encounter with the true self. All the time there has been an absolute reality that is close to us (as close to us as we are to ourselves) and waiting for us to grasp it. And when we do grasp it, we *become* the truth. When the peasant learns that he is a prince, he *becomes* a prince. Viveka does not reply 'oh, how nice', and go back to tilling the soil. No, he quits his plough, puts on silk robes, moves into the palace and then rules over his people. That is what it means to be a prince. And that is what Shankara meant when he taught that knowledge alone will make you happy. When you know your true self, you do not simply file away that knowledge in your mind; you live it out, just as Viveka lived out the knowledge of his royal birth. This is the core of *jnana yoga*: the discovery that wisdom flows effortlessly into action, like a river pouring itself into the sea.

Traditionally, the *jnana yogins* renounce society and give up their family, home, property and career. Because they have learned to discriminate between the world of false appearances and the world of absolute reality, they gladly forsake the world of appearances. For who would choose to live in ignorance and delusion when knowledge and clarity are possible? (To offer a pedestrian analogy, this must feel something like the connoisseur whose refined palate makes the house red undrinkable.) The busy life of the householder – providing for a family, punching the time-clock, being a good neighbour – distracts them from the contemplation of eternal truth, which has become their heart's desire. The wisest seek refuge in a separate realm where other people's ignorance will not stain the purity of their wisdom. (This is not as far-fetched as it seems, for in the medieval Christian West monasteries and universities were created for much the same purpose, although that purpose has now all but disappeared.) We must imagine the recluse to be happy – happier, in fact, than those of us still imprisoned by our delusions in the bustle and business of life.

And yet something in us refuses to pay the price of seclusion for our happiness. This is too cold, too lonely, a view of life, and one that does not serve the demands of the modern world. We insist that happiness must involve others; that it *means* a certain kind of relation-ship with others. In defence of that view we would be quick to point out that the way of knowledge is the least trodden path to happiness. Unarguably, few among us are willing to go (capable of going?) to such extremes to find happiness. We are not all *jnana yogins*, nor do we wish to be.

But that is our problem, and it reveals more about us – our weak-nesses, our fears or perhaps just the circumstances that press upon us from all sides – than it does about happiness. For the *jnana yogin* there is no problem at all. His exceptional life does not feel excep-tional because it is the fitting response to the insight he has gained. We cannot grasp such profound wisdom and expect that our life will remain unchanged, for it is the nature of wisdom to change us. Why, else, do we seek it?

Take up your arrows

In 1962 Indian astrologers calculated that the sun, the moon, the earth and five other planets were about to form an ominous conjunction. So ominous that it might herald the end of the world. Something had to be done, and quickly. It fell to the Brahmins, as guardians of Hindu religious ritual, to organise elaborate prayer services, with millions of holy mantras recited across the country for several weeks. At the predicted moment, the stars and planets moved into the fateful conjunction. And then ... nothing happened.

The scientific explanation was that astrology is nonsense, and so there never was any threat of global annihilation. Perhaps, who knows? The spiritual explanation, and the more appealing one, was that the ritual actions organised by the Brahmins produced enough good karma to ward off the impending disaster. If nothing had been done, the planet *would* have been destroyed. The lesson is that we save the world through work; and in so doing, we save ourselves. Such is *karma yoga*, the way of duty. For Westerners, it is probably the preferred path to happiness, the one that suits the temper of our time.

More than any other Hindu scripture, the *Bhagavad Gita* takes up the theme of duty and expresses it as a problem: how, in any circumstance, do we know what action to take? It is fitting that the *Gita* opens with a moment of *inaction*: Prince Arjuna, the young Pandava warrior, does not know whether to join the battle against his cousins, the Kauravas. Both options are equally abhorrent: fighting means slaughtering his own kinsmen; not fighting means renouncing the sacred duty of his caste. It must have been with great trepidation, then, that Arjuna set his bow and arrow upon the ground and declared that he would not fight. And yet at the same time he sought the advice of his friend Krishna. Was he really doing the right thing? he asked. In Arjuna we are meant to see something of ourselves, and that is easy enough. Countless times in life we hesitate on the brink of action, unsure of our next step. So when Krishna goes on to teach Arjuna about the relationship between action and happiness, the lesson is meant for us, too.

Krishna tells Arjuna that he should do his duty and fight the enemy, even though he and the enemy are of the same blood. Arjuna need not fear the treachery of killing his own cousins because the true self – the soul – is immortal, and thus indestructible. Though the body perishes at death, the soul lives on; and in accordance with the cyclical law of karma, it passes into a new body.

But that is a dry, metaphysical proposition, and not one likely to warm anyone's heart. So Krishna decides to hit home, and he tells Arjuna that it would be shameful and unmanly to renounce his obli-gation to fight, to retreat when others bravely advance. To preserve society, Arjuna must uphold the duties of his caste; if he fails, the consequence will be his own misery:

> ... if you will not wage this war prescribed by your duty, then, by casting off both duty and honour, you will bring evil on yourself ... What could cause you greater pain than this? ... Stand up, then ... resolute for the fight.[3]

This line of reasoning persuades Arjuna to pick up his weapons and enter the fray. At last, he is ready for action. But one thing still bothers him: what *attitude* should he have towards his actions? What psycho-logical disposition, to put Arjuna's concern into modern idiom, should he carry on to the battlefield?

Krishna teaches that we *must* act (passivity is never an option) but always with indifference, neither pinning our hopes on one outcome nor desperately seeking to avoid another. Let us be clear: we are not expected, suddenly, to relinquish all desire and motivation for action. It is not desire itself that is harmful – after all, the desire for happiness is still a desire. Rather, we must prevent ourselves from becoming obsessed with the *results* of what happens when we act upon desire. Our goal, then, is detachment from the fruits of our labour, whether gain or loss, praise or blame, joy or sorrow. Holding these worldly concerns at a distance, we shall come to regard them all equally.

(Around the time that the *Gita* was composed, the first Stoic philosophers in ancient Greece were thinking much the same thing.)

In truth, we must look upon ourselves not as the author of our actions, but as the compliant instrument through which they are accomplished. That is one of the *Gita*'s fundamental teachings. Detachment is neither passivity nor resignation but perfect freedom – the freedom to act in whatever way seems best, seems right, for the situation at hand, because we are no longer fixated on the results of our actions. We all experience this freedom in small but meaningful ways. When the woman in front of you on the street drops her glove, you reach down to pick it up and then return it to her. You do not stop to deliberate over your motive or to calculate your chances for a reward. You do the right thing *because* it is right. In that act of courtesy lies perfect freedom.

Such freedom can be fully gained only through discipline, which is the rousing imperative of *karma yoga*. Action without yoga – without control – is idle movement; just spinning your wheels or revving your engine. To give action its ultimate meaning and purpose, we must temper it through the discipline of yoga. 'Stand fast in Yoga,' Krishna commands; '[i]n success and failure be the same and then get busy with your works'. If you are waiting for a marching order for happiness, this is it.

In the modern world, the greatest example of a *karma yogin* is Mahatma Gandhi (1869–1948), whose life nobly exemplified the path of selfless service. As the whole world knows, Gandhi devoted his life to social change through non-violence. Like Arjuna, he performed his duty in a spirit of detachment. But for all his spiritual depth, he was no hermit. In a crusading life, he battled against discrimination (including the longstanding Hindu prejudice against the 'untouchables'), fought for the end of British colonial rule and, after India gained independence, sought a peaceful resolution to the disputes between the country's Hindu and Muslim populations. Less well known, certainly among non-Hindus, is that Gandhi's favourite

book was the *Bhagavad Gita* (which he first read in an *English* transla-
tion by Sir Edwin Arnold). And yet we can hardly be surprised that
someone so passionately committed to action in the world regarded the
Gita – a gospel of action – as the text that transformed his life.

It transformed his death, too. Gandhi was assassinated by a fellow
Hindu who believed that he had taken the side of Muslims in the
violent controversy that erupted over India's birth as an independent
secular state. From that man's perspective, Gandhi had betrayed his
people; but from the perspective of *karma yoga*, Gandhi had fulfilled
his duty exceptionally well. Transcending factions and sectarian
concerns, he sought the good of all humanity. He lived and died
the truth that peace and harmony should prevail among all people
because all of us are united in the essential oneness of being. Through
his heroic actions, and for the world to see, Gandhi embodied the
abstract principle that the differences between people, however
seemingly indomitable, are mere illusions; and that to hurt another
is to hurt yourself. That a Hindu should have murdered Gandhi is
the sadly ironic testament that he had truly achieved the liberation of
detachment from the consequences of action, and the happiness to
which that detachment unerringly leads.

But not all examples can (or should) be quite so staggering. It is
not difficult to see why in Indian society the inherent practicality of
karma yoga – 'get busy with your works' – appeals to the vast number
of people, some extraordinary but most not, who hold down jobs,
teach their children, honour their parents and serve their communities. Although the householder works, ultimately, for the benefit of
all humanity (as when the Brahmins enacted rituals to ward off the
destruction of the planet), he recognises that even a small, seemingly
insignificant action can be a form of service well rendered. *Any*
worthwhile activity, however ordinary – but done in the right spirit
– takes us one step closer to happiness. And since action confronts
us as at every moment and at every turn, the chance to be happy
is always and everywhere close to hand, found in the steadiness of

heart we bring to every new day, with all its looming crises and surprising adventures.

This is an encouraging lesson, and one widely applicable, since so many of us, Hindu or not, would consider ourselves ordinary householders. And it is no self-disparagement to say that, by and large, we are ordinary. Indeed it is a good thing, since life would be unmanageable if we were all extraordinary. So if we are searching for a general truth about happiness, the Hindu scriptures tell us this: we can find happiness in the life that we already have.

Elephants drinking milk

Within the rich panoply of Hindu gods, Ganesha is one of the most beloved. This elephant-headed deity, worshipped for his power to remove the obstacles we face in life, is an uncommon being. His mother, the goddess Pavarti, created him to guard her while she bathed. One day, her husband, the god Shiva, attempted to intrude into her private chamber. Obedient to his mother's wishes, Ganesha barred his way. Shiva, furious at being prevented from seeing Pavarti – and unaware that Ganesha was his own son – cut off the boy's head. Remorseful upon learning the truth, the god vowed to restore his son to life by giving him the head of the first creature that passed by. Not unusually (for India, that is), this turned out to be an elephant.

Today, whether at home or in temples, many Hindus worship icons of Ganesha, typically small porcelain figures. Through the transforming power of ritual, an icon becomes inhabited by the god whose form it depicts (and thus is much more than a statue, which is merely a lifeless resemblance). When a deity is manifest in an icon it must, like a favourite houseguest, be looked after and cared for; to neglect the icon would be to spurn the god that dwells within it. And so icons are offered food, water, flowers, clothing, incense and, especially, praise and love. Ganesha's devotees often give him spoonfuls of milk. (About a decade ago, a miracle occurred when icons of Ganesha around the world suddenly began to actually drink the milk offered to them.) When devotees attend, in these and similar ways, to the needs of their particular god, they are not engaging in a form of make-believe, let alone lunacy. They are practising *bhakti yoga*. They are finding happiness through loving devotion.

Of all the ways in Hindu culture to find happiness, love is the sweetest and most glorious. It is also the most agreeably human because it begins with something that exists naturally within all of us: the capacity – the need – to love and to be loved in return. *Bhakti* arouses and nourishes this capacity for love, enabling us to reveal unsuspected depths of feeling. In the Hindu tradition those feelings of loving devotion are directed not towards humanity in general, not even another person, but towards god alone. It is helpful to remember that the word *bhakti* derives from the Sanskrit root *bhaj*, meaning 'to be attached to' and 'to have recourse to'. Much more dynamic, more personal, than mere worship, *bhakti* means relying upon a god – taking refuge in him – for protection, assistance or some other benefit. Hence, *bhaktas* organise themselves into sects according to the particular god they worship, such as Vishnu, Shiva, Devi or Ganesha.

Traditionally, the practise of *bhakti yoga* has centred not just on icons but also on temples, shrines, festivals and processions. Sometimes, however, this ancient path takes a surprisingly modern turn. A television adaptation of the *Ramayana*, one of the most famous Hindu epics, attracted an audience of nearly 100 million when it aired in India in the late 1980s. Watching the programme's fifty-two episodes became, in itself, an act of loving devotion towards the god Rama. (The line between appearance and reality quickly blurred as the actors became identified with the gods they portrayed. Some spectators, going to extremes, lined up at the television studio to touch the actors' feet and secure a blessing.[4]) In the West, the most famous *bhakti* movement – and one that for many people is their dominant image of Hinduism – is Hare Krishna (the International Society for Krishna Consciousness, or ISKCON).

Whatever form it takes – feeding icons, watching television, touching feet or parading with tambourines – *bhakti yoga* is all about direct emotional encounters. In one parable, the *bhakta* is compared to a man who, finding himself in a mango orchard, does not cautiously examine each piece of fruit, noting its size, colour, and weight, but simply plucks it from the tree and eats it.[5] Instead of appraising happiness from a distance, he reaches out and grasps it. This is a path to happiness that suits us just fine.

The path of loving devotion is direct, but still it proceeds by steps and stages: listening to and telling stories about the god, chanting his name, remembering and venerating him, making offerings to his image (like the spoonfuls of milk fed to Ganesha), considering yourself his slave, being his friend and, finally, surrendering yourself to him. Self-surrender is the highest act, the supreme example of making one's entire life a gift to god. Nothing else expresses so perfectly the devotee's absolute love because it means being helpless before god, submitting to him utterly and trusting in his protection.

The *Bhagavata Puranas*, a Hindu scripture composed more than a thousand years ago, speak of *bhakti yoga*'s all-consuming nature, when every physical and emotional resource is enlisted for devotion (here, to the god Vishnu):

> Human ears that do not listen to the exploits of Vishnu are mere holes. A tongue that does not sing the songs of Vishnu is as bad as the tongue of a frog ... Hands, even those with flashy gold bracelets, that do not worship Vishnu are the hands of a corpse. Human eyes that do not see the emblems of Vishnu are of no more use than the eyes of a peacock's tail ... A heart that is not moved by hearing Vishnu's names is a heart of stone.[6]

This complete 'giving over' of yourself in loving devotion – we have ears so that we may hear Vishnu, tongues to praise him, eyes to see him, hands to worship him and hearts to be moved by him – is the pure essence of *bhakti yoga*, and what links it to other yogic practices.

All the types of yoga that we are looking at teach the value of detach-ment from what confronts us in the here and now – the world and its demands (*jnana yoga*), action and its consequences (*karma yoga*) and the self and its ego-driven obsessions (*bhakti yoga*) – for in detachment they find the secret of happiness.

The *Bhagavad Gita*, despite its emphasis on duty, affirms that happiness can also be attained through loving devotion. *Bhakti* gathers momentum throughout the *Gita*, and comes into its own near the poem's end, when Krishna bestows upon Arjuna a 'celestial eye' that enables him to behold Krishna in his true supernatural form as the god Vishnu. Krishna declares that only those 'loyal-in-love' to him can ever witness such a vision. In return for such exclusive love, he promises happiness: an end to the karmic cycle of birth, death and rebirth. 'These [my devotees] will I lift up on high out of the ocean of recurring death ... thenceforth in very truth in Me you will find your home'.

Compassionately, Krishna allows anyone to worship him, regard-less of caste or gender. 'For whosoever makes Me his haven, base-born though he may be, yes, women too and artisans, and serfs, theirs it is to tread the highest way'. This is more radical than we may suspect, for within the context of the highly stratified and traditional society for which the *Gita* was composed, it is profoundly liberating to declare that *anyone* can attain happiness.

But how, exactly? Apart from a famous verse that mentions offerings of flowers and recitation of holy texts, the *Gita* does not spell out specific ritual actions. Of course that is not its purpose. The *Gita*'s purpose is to proclaim that *any* action will contribute to our happiness, as long as it is performed in a spirit of loving devotion. Then, the chosen god will free his devotee from the cycle of rebirth and so release him into eternal bliss. Krishna's command – '[w]hatever you do ... offer it up to Me' – is thus also a promise – 'those who commune with me in love's devotion [abide] in Me, and I in them'.

Here again we see Hinduism's reassuring inclusivity. You need not search for extraordinary ways to show your love because the right ways are all around you: '*whatever* you do, offer it up to Me'. If your love is pure then your beloved will be pleased, whatever you do; if your heart is in the right place then happiness will be yours, whatever your life is like. Yet without the right disposition you will *never* find happiness, no matter how exhaustive your effort. 'You may thrust your head into all the corners of the world,' Swami Vivekananda taught a century ago, 'you may explore the Himalayas, the Alps and the Caucasus … you will not find it [bliss] anywhere until your heart is ready for receiving it.'[7]

Frequently the relationship between the devotee and his god develops into a passionate fixation, sometimes bordering on obsession. The *Bhakti Sutras*, an ancient collection of sayings, tells us that the *bhakta* feels 'joy in His [the deity's] presence, pain in His absence, indifference toward other objects'.[8] How far away we have moved from the cool rationalism of *jnana yoga* and the earnest practicality of *karma yoga*. Happiness now arises as an overpowering, incomparable experience of joy. We have entered the realm of ecstasy; and with ecstasy comes risk. The risk is that the devotee will succumb to sentimentality, eroticism or zealotry. Intense emotions play a vital role in *bhakti yoga*, but they must be the right sort of emotions; otherwise, the devotee might cross the line that separates the lover from the lunatic. As ever, the way to keep matters under control is through detachment from desire.

Bhakti yoga does not find easy expression in modern secular society. But, still, there are lessons that Westerners can take away from ritual practices that they are unlikely to adopt in their own lives. The greatest lesson must be that the way of love, no less than the ways of knowledge and duty, directs us to be detached. In *bhakti yoga* there is no room for self-indulgent emotion because the emotions that count are not ours, but god's. For god's sake alone do we express our love, and not for any rapture that we might thereby obtain. We want strong feelings and we want to express them unashamedly; but the whole point of releasing such feelings is to let them direct us somewhere else; to give our life a focal point on the distant horizon. Love, because it is selfless, carries us beyond ourselves and into a vaster, possibly infinite, reality. When that happens, our immediate concern for ourselves drops away like leaves falling off a tree. Thus, Krishna reserves his love only for

> the man who hates not nor exults, who mourns not nor desires, who puts away both pleasant and unpleasant things ... I love the man who is the same to friend and foe, [the same] whether he be respected or despised, the same in heat and cold, in pleasure as in pain, who has put away attachment and remains unmoved by praise or blame ...

These are cool words for the fiery art of love. Paradoxical though it seems, we learn once again that happiness lies in freedom from desire. But perhaps the greater paradox is that love, so often confused with, or at least wrapped up in, desire, gives us the strength to 'put away attachment' and overcome our fixation with how the world sees us.

On the street where you live
In the introduction we touched upon the question of whether there is anything to be gained from understanding happiness in terms of someone else's beliefs. Now we must face it head on, because for many readers (at least those reading from start to finish) this will be the first chapter in which they encounter a religious tradition other than their own. Some will claim no such tradition, others will look warily on those who do. All that is to be expected, and does not in itself derail the book's progress nor throw into doubt and confusion the reader's engagement with it. We all can understand (as distinct from accept) things we do not believe, or even tolerate.

The problem, if problem it be, with Hindu perspectives on happiness is that, despite being found the world over, Hinduism is still a local and ethnic religion. Although one in seven people on the planet are Hindus, nearly all of them live in India, and those who live elsewhere are almost exclusively from Indian families. Hinduism (unlike its cousin, Buddhism) has never been a missionary religion, and converts are rare. It is tied, inextricably and exclusively, to the culture and society of South Asia. Does this limit the insights that it might convey to people outside a prescribed set of born believers?

Hinduism's strong roots in Indian culture mean that it focuses on worldliness. Not that it teaches attachment to worldly goods (it does not), but that it teaches *how to live in the world*: how to do your duty, express your love, raise a family, help your neighbour, pursue wealth and manage a career. Hinduism is less a set of doctrines and dogmas than a way of life (here, the contrast with Christianity and Islam could not be stronger). Certainly it has philosophical systems and abstract concepts, but its real richness lies in its diverse rituals, traditions and devotional practices. Devotees of the god Krishna worship him by offering water, food and flowers to his icon. The Hindu *pandit*, or storyteller, spends years memorising several hundred thousand verses of sacred scriptures so that he can recite them to the faithful. People bathe in the sacred river Ganges because of its sanc-tifying and purifying powers. These are all examples of how good Hindus should act.

And action takes precedence over belief. That is really what distinguishes East from West. Eastern religions focus on the individu-al's search or quest, Western ones on the object of belief. The Hindu asks, 'What must I *do* to be saved?'; the Christian and the Muslim ask, 'What must I *believe* to be saved?' Hindus emphasise behaviour, social rules and ritual because they give meaning to virtually every aspect of life. Meaning is woven into life's very fabric. Through its worldly disposition – 'get busy with your works', as Krishna commanded Arjuna – Hinduism makes common cause with people of other faiths or of none. That is how an ethnic religion speaks to a global audience and how the secret of its ancient wisdom about happiness is, in truth, an open one.

4

The Enlightened One
(Buddhism)

Prince Siddhartha Gautama (*c.* 566–486 BC), known to history as the Buddha, was born in Kapilavatthu, near the foothills of the Himalayas, just across the border of present-day Nepal. His birth, like that of Jesus Christ, was heralded by miracles. He was conceived when his mother, Queen Maya, dreamt that a white baby elephant with a lotus flower in its trunk entered her side. Royal astrologers interpreted the dream as a sign of the child's auspicious yet uncertain future: if he remained at court, he would become a great conquering warrior; but if he grew discontented with courtly life, he would leave and become a great spiritual leader. King Suddhodana, determined that his son would succeed him, consulted the astrologers once more: 'How can I keep my child from leaving the royal palace?' They replied that the boy must be forever shielded from the sight of anything ugly or unpleasant. Luxury must be his entire world. Thus insulated from cold reality, he would never leave his fantasy world because he would never know that it was a fantasy.

At the moment the child was born, the earth trembled and the heavens sent down a shower of water to bathe him. Miraculously, he stood up, took seven steps (a lotus blossomed under his foot with each step) and declared; 'I have been born to achieve awakening for the good of the world; this is my last birth.' Though but an infant, he had come to the end of the karmic cycle of reincarnation. In recognition of this marvel the child was named Siddhartha Gautama, 'he who has achieved his goal'.

Heeding the warnings of the astrologers, Suddhodana imprisoned his newborn son in splendour. For many years, the king's elaborate deception succeeded, and Siddhartha lived an idyllic life, free from the disquieting knowledge that people grow old, feel pain and die. But one day when the prince rode his chariot outside the palace, he saw something horrifying and strange: an old man. 'Why,' he asked his charioteer, 'does the man look so sad?' Because old age is a burden, the servant replied. Siddhartha, realising that he, too, shared the old man's fate, returned home in unaccustomed melancholy to contemplate the suffering of advancing years. The strange sights multiplied. On his next journey he saw a sick man. On his third journey he witnessed a corpse being carried to a cremation ground. And then Siddhartha witnessed the vision that would transform him: a religious mendicant, a poor holy man dressed in yellow robes who wandered from town to town, surviving on the charity of strangers.

In a flash of insight, Siddhartha knew that he must do the same. That night he stole out of his father's palace, vowing to find a new, more meaningful life among the religious ascetics who dwelt in the dense forests. He left the palace on horseback and stopped when he reached the bank of a river. There, in a ritual of symbolic rebirth, he unbridled his horse, shaved his head and beard and exchanged clothes with a passing stranger. Siddhartha, on the outside as well as the inside, was a new man. It was the start of a great adventure – the 'going forth'.

The lesson of the story of the four sights is that we delude ourselves about the truth of life. The palace, that vast protective world, shields Siddhartha from true reality. Hiding inside it, he lives a comfortable, yet essentially artificial life. But he fails to realise its artificiality because he cannot imagine anything else. Until the chariot ride. The chariot ride is the breakthrough moment, the moment when Siddhartha shatters the barrier of delusion and for the first time sees the true nature of reality. But what he sees is unexpectedly brutal and bleak: we grow old, we suffer, we die.

We, too, are trapped by false beliefs, and do not even know that we are trapped. Such is the core teaching of Buddhism. But if we are ready for it, what lies ahead is the mental journey (our modern-day chariot ride) from delusion to insight and, finally, to wisdom. Which is another way of saying that it is a journey to happiness. Like Siddhartha, we can delay the journey only for so long. Something inside us – call it the dark night of the soul, a change of heart, or even a mid-life crisis, so little does the label matter – compels us to leave the palace, climb into the chariot and take to the open road. So might begin our own adventure of going forth.

Under the fig tree

Jolted out of complacency, Siddhartha spent the next six years in a quest for spiritual knowledge that he called 'The Great Renunciation'. There was nothing exceptional about his quest, for we must imagine the forests of northern India populated by monks in yellow robes, all of them begging for food, seeking wisdom and blazing a spiritual trail. At first, Siddhartha practised meditation, mysticism, fasting and other ascetic rituals. But it was to no avail, and he came to realise that the path to enlightenment was the proverbial 'middle way', and not the dangerous avenues of extravagance and deprivation that lay on either side. Judiciously, we must steer a course between too much and not enough. Years later, he likened the 'middle way' to a perfectly tuned lute whose strings were neither too tight nor too loose.

Siddhartha embarked upon the middle path by staying still: he sat under a huge fig tree and began to meditate. In his honour, the tree came to be known as the Bodhi tree, or 'Tree of Awakening'. For it was underneath that tree, on a night when the full moon shone in the month of Vaisakha, that Siddhartha woke up to the truth of all things. By sunrise he understood that for him the karmic cycle had come to its end, just as he had prophesied thirty-five years earlier on the day he was born. Having for ever expelled desire and ignorance from his life, he was released into the eternal happiness known as nirvana. In that transforming moment, Prince Siddhartha, like a flame that is blown out, ceased to be. There was only the Buddha, the enlightened one.

Out of compassion for the suffering of all humanity, the Buddha (for so he must now be called) dedicated the rest of his life to sharing his teaching – the *Dharma* – with the world. Knowing that his mission was too large to undertake by himself, he travelled to a deer park outside Benares where he rejoined five of his fellow religious mendicants. There, in the company of his earliest followers, Buddha declared himself a *tathagata* – 'one who has arrived at what is so' – and preached the sermon (*sutra*) that first revealed to the world the Four Noble Truths and the Eightfold Path. As the five disciples listened, they, too, gained enlightenment and were ordained the first Buddhist monks. The mission was underway.

For the remaining forty-five years of his life, Buddha preached to a growing number of followers in surrounding villages and towns of northern India. It was during his own lifetime that monasteries were established, often by local kings or rich merchants, to provide shelter for the Buddha and his disciples when monsoons prevented them from travelling. And so the custom developed that during the summer rainy season, the monks remained together for a spiritual retreat. The monastery served not just as a welcome refuge but also, and more importantly, as a living model for enlightenment; a beacon shining in a dark world. As a place where monks and nuns lived and worked alongside the laity, it beautifully symbolised the middle way: neither totally absorbed within society, nor completely severed from it. Even today, thousands of years later, life in a Buddhist monastery remains a rare and precious image of what the world would be like if everyone attained spiritual fulfilment.

In his eightieth year, the Buddha died peacefully in a grove of trees just outside the small and obscure town of Kusinara. Sensing that his life's journey had come to its end, he calmly prepared himself to cross over to death's far shore. He lay on his right side between two sala trees (the same trees found in the grove where he was born) with his head pointing north and one foot resting upon the other. Miraculously, the sala trees bloomed out of season and showered their petals upon him. It was a sign, Buddha said, that the gods had come to be with him for his final moment of glory. Turning to the five hundred monks who assembled to witness his death, he spoke his last words: 'All things of the world are passing. Strive with a clear mind to reach nirvana.' Slipping into a meditative trance, the Buddha passed through to that perfect nirvana which is the extinction of identity, and its perfection. As he was released from mortal life, the gods smiled, the monks wept, the earth trembled and thunder rolled across the open sky.

The four noble truths

On the moonlit night in spring that he reached enlightenment, the Buddha found release from suffering because he had ended the seemingly endless karmic cycle of birth, death and rebirth. His example teaches us that we, too, can free ourselves from suffering in this life (although the task is far from easy). What Buddha taught about suffering – and the overcoming of it – has been long known as the Four Noble Truths:

- The Truth of Suffering
- The Truth of Arising
- The Truth of Cessation
- The Truth of the Path

These sweetly reasonable truths disclose the reality of suffering, its cause, its cure and the path that leads to the cure. Like a doctor whose patient is all humanity, Buddha diagnoses our common illness (suffering), determines its root cause (desire), finds the radical cure (suffering can end) and then prescribes it (the path that leads to the end of suffering). These truths are noble because they enhance spiritual development and help us progress towards the happiness that is nirvana. They are noble in purpose. Yet beyond that, it takes a nobility of character to let yourself focus on suffering in the world, and not be distracted by desire's siren song.

The truth of suffering

To put Buddhism's central truth in one sentence: life is suffering. That is what Prince Siddhartha learned on his chariot ride when he saw an old man, a sick man, a poor man and a dead man. There are many ways to suffer, for suffering afflicts both the body and the mind. Death, pain, infirmity and disease are merely the most visible forms of suffering. Less apparently, though perhaps more damagingly, we suffer feelings of grief, frustration and despair; we suffer negative mental states, such as greed, hatred and addiction; we suffer, even in times of seeming contentment, boredom and anxiety. Our families are infuriating. Our friends let us down. Our pastimes are no longer pleasurable.

In these ways, suffering infects the totality of life. So much is it a part of life that suffering accompanies even joyful events. The birth of a child – surely, an occasion to celebrate – turns out to be yet another type of suffering because it places the innocent newborn in a world of disappointment and pain. We are born astride a grave, as Samuel Beckett wrote in his famously despairing play *Waiting for Godot*. Every instant of life takes us closer to death, and neither hard work nor good fortune will save us from that inevitable fate. The truth of suffering is the profoundly unsettling awareness that discontent is our constant companion, our intimate partner, in the journey through life.

How can such a dark and despairing vision have anything to do with happiness? we find ourselves asking. Yet to put it that way is to ask the wrong question (one that 'does not fit the case', as Buddha would say) because the question itself presumes that the truth of suffering is pessimistic, when in fact it is no such thing. The truth is what it is, and to see things as they really are is the first step towards happiness. Buddhism does not try to persuade you to be optimistic about life, or dissuade you from being pessimistic, for those are false choices. Rather, it invites you to be realistic, which is the only honest response. A truly pessimistic response would be to run away from suffering, to deny its existence. But a more helpful and classically Buddhist approach is to accept the truth of suffering in a heartfelt way. Like Siddhartha in his chariot, we must allow the truth of suffering, sober and cheerless though it is, not to harden us but soften us. Yes, there is suffering in the world – now let's do something about it. For unless we show compassion for the plight of others we have no hope of winning happiness for ourselves.

The truth of arising

The law of karma tells us that everything has a cause. Buddha called this the principle of 'dependent arising': everything that arises in the world is the consequence of, and thus dependent upon, something that preceded it. Suffering arises in the world, and its cause is desire. Desire is what causes us to be reborn in this world of suffering, and only when we stand apart from our desires can we, finally, escape suffering.

Some desires are sharply focused, and we seek whatever is gratifying to taste, to touch or to see. Strawberries and cream. Silk against the skin. Scarlett Johannson. Other desires feel more like inner compulsions. Buddha described this as an excessive attachment to life. He meant an insatiable drive to experience new things; to race through life with your foot pressing on the accelerator. Most of all, he meant a desire to become someone other (not someone better, which is entirely different) than the person you are right now.

In Western culture, a vivid image for headstrong desire is Faust: the man who sold his immortal soul to the devil in exchange for twenty-four years of unmatched knowledge and power. Faust desired to live more intensely than anyone in history; and having fulfilled that desire, he paid for it with the price of eternal damnation. Like all tragic figures, he realised his error only when it was too late to make amends. Although Buddha would not have accepted the story's Christian framework, he would nonetheless have endorsed its lesson: that the desire – if we indulge it – to take more from life than is our proper share, our allotted portion, will bring us only to grief.

The truth of cessation

Yet we are not doomed to bear our burdens for ever. There is a cure for suffering, and the cure is freedom from desire. The *Dhammapada*, a collection of Buddhist scriptures from the third century BC, teaches that 'whoever in this world overcomes his selfish cravings, his sorrows fall away from him, like drops of water from a lotus flower'.[1] This is the Truth of Cessation: our suffering ceases when our desires are overcome.

Buddhism invites us to meditate upon suffering not to be demoralised about it, not to be consumed by it, but to be released from it. Far from being mysterious, the cure for our suffering is plainly rational: to end suffering we must remove its cause, which is desire. The logic of the thing may be easily grasped, but the doing of it is not so simple. But it is crucial to understand what we are being called to do. To seek enlightenment does not mean that we seek (as an Epicurean would) to remove the physical pain and stressful moments of normal, everyday life. That would be to deny life its due – even the Buddha died in pain. What enlightenment *does* remove is the mental and emotional anguish that too often threatens to take control of our life; to take possession of it, like a thief in the empty house that is us. The liberation that we seek lies in altering not life itself (that would take a miracle, which is not our line of work) but our reaction and response to it.

Among Westerners, scepticism is a common reaction to the Truth of Cessation. While most of us would accept that curbing excess is a good and useful thing, we would be quick to point out that some desires are legitimate and so should *not* be conquered. The desire for food, clothing and shelter are so basic that without them life is unsustainable. Even the desire for enlightenment is still a desire. So how does the Truth of Cessation make sense for everyday life? Not just for survival, but for a life enriched by meaning and purpose? The answer hinges on the difference between deprivation and detachment.

A few years ago, a mendicant Buddhist nun living in Hertfordshire, Sister Kovinda, told her story to the journalist Vicki Mackenzie, who was researching a book on Buddhist converts in the West. (Mackenzie's fascinating book, published in 2003, is called *Why Buddhism?*) Sister Kovinda spoke candidly of how she wrestled with hunger, that most animalistic desire. The rules of her order stipulate that each day the nuns must eat their main meal out of the 'alms bowl'; instead of buying or preparing food, they must rely upon whatever they receive.

On many days this strict requirement is met through food donated by lay people visiting the monastery. But on less bountiful days, the nuns must leave the monastery, walk into the village and do a 'round' on the streets. Sister Kovinda cannot ask for food (let alone for anything particular), nor can she accept money. She might be given a teacake, a sandwich or nothing at all. What she eats – *whether* she eats – depends entirely upon the generosity of strangers. The ritual of the begging round is not a punishment but something that serves a socially unifying purpose: the laity earn good karma by showing charity while the monks and nuns receive alms that aid their search for nirvana.

To endure this ordeal – how else can so uncertain an experience be described? – Sister Kovinda detaches herself from her desire for food, whether a chocolate biscuit (for which she confesses a fondness) or any food at all. She sets her desires to one side. In a practised spirit of detachment, she expects nothing yet remains grateful for whatever she receives. If nothing comes her way, she does not let herself become anxious. Rather, she stays calm by thinking to herself, 'I'll be fine if I don't eat … I'm not going to die if I don't eat today.'[2] If her desire is satisfied, she is content; if it is not satisfied, still she is content. That is what it means to conquer desire: to treat it with indifference.

What comes across in the interview is Sister Kovinda's honesty. There is no saintly pretence that she does not feel hunger and cravings. Such feelings are human, and so there is no reason to be ashamed of them. But what emerges even more forcefully is her canniness. This street-smart nun knows the best places to conduct her 'rounds'; she can spot the people most likely to offer her something, and she knows exactly what types of food will give her enough energy to get through the day. There is nothing otherworldly about her. Just the opposite: no one could be more harnessed to the reality of her situation than Sister Kovinda, who every day witnesses acts of charity and selfishness alike. She has answered Buddhism's call to cultivate a more detached attitude towards the things she desires, both what she possesses and what she pursues.

The truth of the path

How, in the intimate details of everyday life, do we lift our conscious-ness to a level where all these noble truths are shown to be true, so that within life we can create our own happiness? Buddha's answer was the Eightfold Path: a guide for adapting our behaviour in everyday life so that we will move from suffering and rebirth to the cessation of suffering and, finally, to nirvana. The path encompasses the full spectrum of human excellence, which Buddha described as wisdom (knowing things), morality (acting virtuously) and meditation (developing healthy attitudes). This is the path that leads straight to happiness.

Each of the eight steps in the path tells us what our beliefs, actions and attitudes should be. Wisdom, for example, means (among other things) 'right action': realising the impermanence of all things; morality means (again, among other things) 'right livelihood': not having an occupation that causes harm to others or to the world;

meditation means 'right effort': controlling our thoughts so that they can be used for good purposes, such as resisting temptation. Buddha did not claim to have invented the path, for it had been there all along; it was of ancient origin, and others, in distant times, had walked it before him. He claimed only to have remembered what had been long forgotten.

When Buddha encouraged his disciples to perform 'right' actions or to cultivate 'right' beliefs and attitudes, he was not referring to any rules or laws handed down from on high. Buddha was no Moses on Mount Sinai, carrying down to his people the sacred tablets on which God himself carved the Ten Commandments. That kind of legal- istic thinking would not have made sense to Buddha, who believed that actions are 'right' not because they conform to an established rule (no such rule exists) but because they move us forward on the path to happiness. It can be difficult for Westerners to understand that, from a Buddhist perspective, to be 'right' means not to comply with an externally imposed rule, but to live your life, in ways both large and small, with dexterity and skill.

So instead of commanding his disciples to follow the Eightfold Path, Buddha invited them to judge for themselves whether 'right actions' made sense in their own lives; whether such actions were useful in achieving enlightenment. If they are useful, continue with them; if not, find other ones. From its earliest days down to the present one, Buddhism has freely adapted itself to the changing shape and pattern of individual lives. That is exactly what Buddha himself would have wished, he once compared his teachings to a sheet of gold that we are free to shape into a cloak that fits us perfectly.

In a paradox typically Buddhist, the Eightfold Path is both a path and not a path. It is a path because it leads from one place to another: from suffering to happiness. But it is not a path because it lacks a strict sequence. The eight steps – understanding, resolve, speech, action, livelihood, effort, mindfulness and meditation – are not stages to be passed through in a pre-determined order. Rather, they are the basic tasks of life that, time and again, we must work through. So they are not steps but the occasions for action in the world. Never can we put them behind us, for their challenge is always there, confronting us in life's every moment. Nor do they come upon us in a peaceful and ordered way. They rise up all at once, in a great riotous onslaught, and we tackle them as best we can.

Nirvana

At the end of the path to happiness, nirvana awaits. Stepping off the Wheel of Life, we escape, once and for ever, the imprisoning cycle of birth, death and rebirth. That sense of escape, of leaving something behind, is crucial for our understanding. When Buddha spoke of nirvana, he preferred to use negative images – a lack of desire, a thirst slaked, a flame that goes out. Indeed, nirvana's literal meaning is 'to extinguish' or 'to blow out'. What all Buddhist teachings convey is that nirvana is an experience of *not*: *not* being chained to desire, *not* having attachments and, therefore, *not* suffering. To quote from a famous Buddhist scripture, nirvana is 'not a coming, not a going, nor a standing still, nor a falling, nor a rising'.

Instead of thinking of nirvana as entering into a new state, we should think of it as being released from an old one. What you are released into is beside the point. The point is that you are no longer where you once were. Buddhists use various images to convey this sense of release, of going beyond. One text likens nirvana to a fresh flower rising out of muddy water. Another says that a person who attains nirvana is like a bird escaping a net. The only thing that matters is to be set free, to no longer be trapped in the net. Most commonly, nirvana is described as a fire that has gone out; and to reach it means to extinguish the blaze of desire that rages inside us. Thus, Buddha spoke of the 'coolness' of nirvana, for it turns down desire's broiling heat.

The happiness of nirvana can be reached in this (or a future) life, but only rarely in a full or complete way. The model is Buddha himself, who achieved both nirvana-in-this-life (when he meditated under the Bodhi tree) and the perfect nirvana attained only at death (when he was released from the cycle of rebirth). Nirvana in this life is an actual occurrence, and one that lies within our power. It is a complete transformation of personality characterised by peace, compassion and joy. Negative thoughts, worries and anxieties are expelled from an enlightened mind. Of course there are degrees to this ongoing process, and those of us still searching for enlightenment can attain some of nirvana's attributes. Only a fully enlightened person, however, can possess them completely.

The time scale for enlightenment is long term in the extreme, and thus uncongenial to the modern ethos of instant gratification. If you ask Buddhists whether they expect to attain nirvana in this life, they would almost certainly answer 'no'. But they might well raise an eyebrow or let a smile sneak across their face, because the question itself betrays a confusion about the search for enlightenment, as if it were one more item to be checked off on a 'to do' list. Most Buddhists would not believe that they hover on the brink of nirvana, and will cross the final threshold any moment now. More pragmatically, they would be concerned with accumulating merit – good karma – through selfless service and compassion, thereby winning a better rebirth in the next life. And with each successive life, they will move ever closer to the ultimate goal of nirvana. But when, at last, that longed for moment occurs, it will occur in actual life. Just like Buddha under the Tree of Awakening, they will have their own moment of blissful transfiguration.

Unlike Jews, Christians and Muslims, Buddhists do not believe in an afterlife. They believe that when people die, they are reborn. Except for the person who achieves enlightenment. So what happens to an enlightened person at death? As Buddha himself would say, that is the wrong question to ask, because 'it does not tend to edification'. Merely to pose the question is to court confusion. Wondering what becomes of an enlightened person at death, Buddha taught, is like wondering what becomes of a flame that is snuffed out. Nothing *becomes* of it: the flame has not gone somewhere else; it is simply no more. Just as the flame dies when starved of oxygen, the flame of suffering dies when starved of desire. There is no 'I' who attains nirvana, because nirvana means the extinction of the selfish, all-consuming 'I'.

Imagine a man wounded by a poisoned arrow. Rather than simply removing the arrow, he asks 'Who shot me?', 'Where is he from?', 'What kind of bow did he use?'. By asking these irrelevant questions the wounded man is only making a bad situation worse: the arrow is still piercing his flesh, still releasing poison into his bloodstream. This man, says Buddha, is the man who wastes his life speculating about nirvana. Instead of advancing him along the path to enlightenment, his pointless questions block his way. So the lesson is clear: if you want to attain happiness through nirvana, then go ahead. Walk on. 'Move and the Way will open to you.' But stop asking questions that do not fit the case. And pluck the poisoned arrow of suffering from your side.

If you see Buddha, kill him

Always a missionary religion, although never, like Christianity and Islam, a conquering one, Buddhism has spread far beyond the towns and villages of northern India where twenty-five centuries ago the Buddha himself first preached. It became the first world religion, travelling along trade routes – the fabled 'Silk Road' to China – over mountaintops and across seas. As it migrated, initially throughout the Indian subcontinent and then to all of Asia, from Afghanistan to Japan, Buddhism developed into a number of schools and fashioned itself according to the local customs and traditions of the various cultures that it encountered. It took a much longer time for Buddhism to reach the West. Only since the middle of the nineteenth century has this ancient religious tradition, five hundred years older than Christianity, been seriously studied outside Asia. Of more recent occurrence, beginning in the 1960s, has been conversion to Buddhism by Westerners.

In North America and Europe, Buddhism exists not as a single religious entity but as a plurality of congregations, monasteries, temples and study groups, which are known collectively as the *sangha*, 'the community'. Indo-Chinese immigrants – the hundreds of thousands who fled their homeland in the wake of the Vietnam War – founded Buddhist communities throughout the United States, most especially in California. Within these communities, monastery-trained teachers began to instruct Americans in Buddhist practices and beliefs. From this early generation of converts came the first American-born Buddhist teachers and priests. Today, the total Buddhist community (both immigrants and converts) in the United States numbers several million. A similar, though less dramatic, expansion has occurred in the United Kingdom and Western Europe, where more than a million people have converted – most of whom, it should be noted, are drawn from the white liberal educated elite.

When people enter the Buddhist community, whether as monks, nuns or lay people, they take three vows:

- I take refuge in the Buddha
- I take refuge in the *dharma*
- I take refuge in the *sangha*

The Buddha, the *dharma* and the *sangha* are the 'three jewels' of Buddhism: the example, the path and the community. The vow is not a profession of belief but an act of finding protection, sanctuary and peace. To 'take refuge' is to immerse yourself in something greater and beyond yourself, to be sustained and inspired by it. This absence of religious doctrine – a creed – has meant that Buddhism's influence in the West has been more cultural than religious.

But *why* has this ancient religion from the Far East tapped into the popular imagination of the modern secular West? Perhaps that question, too, does not fit the case. Perhaps the better, more timely, question is, Why is the West *now* receptive to Buddhist teachings and practices? Why, at this point in its history, is the West poised to learn from Buddhism in a way that was not possible during periods of Western imperial and religious dominion?

The answer, surely, is that Buddhism strikes a responsive chord with so many of our concerns and values today: distrust of organised religion; demand for rational, scientific explanations; feelings of alienation; and obsession with the cult of the individual. Westerners who accept Buddhism do so sincerely, but they do it primarily to 'repair' themselves – and society at large – by subscribing to Buddhist values. People in the West regard Buddhism as a healing faith, which is starkly different from how they probably regard the Judaeo-Christian heritage: as the preservation of God's revealed word. But the need for healing is so strong that they are willing to go outside their own culture to find it.

As his death drew near, the Buddha considered naming someone to lead the monastic order after he had gone; but he decided there was no need for a successor because he himself had never been a leader. He trusted that the community would take care of itself, and so it has, for more than two millennia. True to its founder's wishes, Buddhism has never recognised a central authority – a rabbi, bishop or ayatollah – on doctrinal matters. It is not a hard-line faith; indeed, it is not a faith at all, for there is no deity to be worshipped (Buddha was a man, not a god) but only the self to be awakened. Far from demanding strict obedience, Buddhism actively encourages questioning – test it out, try it for yourself, see if it works in your own life. One ninth-century Zen master told his students, 'If you meet the Buddha, kill the Buddha!', to underscore the importance of remaining independent of authority figures. The Buddha himself must be the first spiritual leader in history to tell his followers not to accept his teaching just because he gave it to them.

And that is precisely what Buddha meant when he told his disciples to turn his teaching into a golden cloak fashioned for each of them uniquely. He was telling them that the journey to happiness is always an individual, inward journey; not submission to the force of authority or passionate devotion to a charismatic guru but a patient listening to your own thoughts, feelings and hopes. Thus, Buddhism imposes few ritual or sacramental requirements, and is easily adapted to different lifestyles (there are Buddhist diamond merchants, fashion photographers and guitar players). For anyone wary of the power wielded by large religious institutions, Buddhism is reassuringly small. And small, the saying goes, is beautiful.

Western converts to Buddhism praise its intellectual vigour, its clear explanations and its anchored rationality. Almost uncannily, Buddhism seems to have anticipated the longings of modern scientific spiritualists: those who aspire to something beyond this plane of existence, yet also demand a cogent rationale for it. Karma, the universal law of cause and effect, is the perfect solution, for it explains logically how the past, the present and the future are interconnected. Without resorting to either mystery or superstition, Buddhism presents a seamless explanation for how the universe works and for how each of us fits into it.

Buddhism is not so much a 'believing' as a 'doing'; less a faith to be professed than a path to be followed. With no use for authority figures, its only basis is experience: to hear for ourselves the lion's roar of truth. Buddha remained steadfast in the belief that even his own teachings must be tested in the crucible of experience. He did not want anyone simply to take his word for it. It is precisely this emphasis on each person's unique quest for happiness that makes Buddhism so much at home in the Western cult of the individual.

Yet there is a crucial difference. Our ego may well prompt us to learn more about Buddhism – what can Buddha do for *me*? – but the more we learn, the more we realise that the ego is a trap. To engage with Buddhism (or Hinduism) in any depth is to question the very existence of the 'self' that we are trying to discover. Just who is this *me* that I so desperately want to find? Buddhism's answer is unexpected and strange: there is no enduring self; there is only the self that is continually becoming, ever evolving, always striving. To use a classic Buddhist image: the self is not a pool of stagnant water but a freshly flowing stream. A stream of becoming.

In a way that transcends psychotherapy (to say nothing of popular self-help manuals), which is all about building up the self into a stable whole, Buddhist teachings dismantle the whole project of managing the self and release us from its stranglehold. Of course it is not that the self actually disappears, but that we come to question why so much of our life is held hostage by a pointless attempt to prop up that most cherished, and most fragile, possession: self-image.

Ultimately, though, the secret of Buddhism's popularity in the West lies in its union of spiritual transcendence and activity in the world. It answers a question that has puzzled mankind for millennia: how do you believe in something beyond yourself and yet continue to live in the here-and-now? It is a mistake to imagine that Buddhists are disconnected from the world, *kung fu* masters who speak in riddles or shaven-headed monks dressed in saffron robes. Such appearances are real, but they have nothing to do with passivity – the law of karma sees to that. For the cyclical nature of karma insists that you do only those things that you are willing to do for ever.

This is a formidably high standard to meet. Do you want to lose your temper *for ever*? Wear clothes made by children in sweatshops *for ever*? Pollute the environment *for ever*? You cannot dodge the question by claiming that it will be all right just this once because there is no 'just this once' – that's what karma means. If you accept the law of karma then you cannot wreak havoc and destruction in the world. Through the Buddhist ethic of compassion you transform yourself into someone who does not exploit the world, but fiercely guards it and cares lovingly for it. You take responsibility for the world, recognising that your every action will have untold consequences down the centuries. Detached from desire, the person who is happy holds the world at a distance, so that they may see all the more clearly how to make it better.

Prisons of the soul

Arturo, a young Mexican-American, will spend the rest of his life confined to an 8 x 10 cell in Pelican Bay Prison in northern California. He has already spent more than half his twentysome years in prisons and juvenile detention centres. It was when he was jailed for life that Arturo first learned about Buddhism. His teacher was Robina Courtin, a lesbian feminist Buddhist nun who was the first person to visit him in three years. Arturo later told Sister Robina that Buddhism 'penetrated my heart and slapped me in the face'. In the opposition, almost comically incongruous, between the glow of good feeling and the bracing wake-up call, those two images vividly evoke the shift from inward transformation to outward action. Buddhism begins with self-discovery, but then it rouses you to action, compelling you — with the force of a slap in the face — to seek the good of all creatures.[3]

On the day he turned twenty-one, Arturo received a birthday card from a Buddhist *lama* (teacher) who reminded him that

> [w]e think people who are outside prison are not prisoners, but actually we are. Even people who are travelling the whole world and are regarded as successful, who think they have everything — all the desire objects — actually are in prison, the prison of their inner life, because their inner life is crying, so miserable and unhappy, not finding satisfaction. They are even more unhappy than people who have very little.[4]

It is tempting to imagine how those words were received by a young man serving three life sentences. Did he find them patronising? Did they make him cynical? Compassionate? When Sister Robina visits Arturo, who rises each day at 5 a.m., and whose first words upon awakening are taken from a traditional Buddhist prayer — 'May I use this day for my own benefit and the good of others' — she is convinced that she has come to see a man who is happy. Though there is much to learn from Arturo's conversion to Buddhism, we must not romanticise it; for there is nothing sweet or innocent about it. If he leaves his cell or is given a cellmate, he will be attacked, probably killed, by prisoners who do not understand why this ex-gang member now meditates and reads Buddhist scriptures. His survival depends entirely upon his isolation. Arturo may not be in a prison of the mind, but he is in a prison nonetheless – and one that he is powerless to leave.

Still, we must be wary of opening the door to mere sentimentality. So let me conclude with a story of failure. Robert Thurman is a man of signal accomplishment: the first Westerner to be ordained a Tibetan Buddhist monk (the Dalai Lama supervised his spiritual exercises), a professor of Indo-Tibetan studies at Columbia University and father of actress Uma Thurman. As a philosophy student at Harvard, the young Thurman lost his left eye when a tire iron slipped out of his hand and penetrated his eye socket. At that moment, Thurman, like Prince Siddhartha on his chariot ride, realised his own mortality. It's hard to resist a symbolic reading of the story: the partial loss of outward vision gives rise to a more penetrating inner vision. (In mythology, the blind man – Oedipus, most famously – is the one who sees reality more clearly than everyone else.) The near-fatal accident prompted Thurman to make a pilgrimage to the Middle East and Asia, and it was during this trip that he discovered Tibetan Buddhists living in exile in India. (The Communist Chinese invasion of Tibet in 1950, which ended centuries of rule by successive Dalai Lamas, resulted in a worldwide Tibetan Buddhist diaspora.) Meeting them, he felt he had come home.

Ever since, Thurman has followed the Eightfold Path. Many of those years have been spent in Manhattan, probably the place on earth least conducive to meditation and tranquillity. Still, the path is there, waiting to be walked. What is most admirable about Thurman is neither his vast knowledge nor his wide-ranging expertise, nor even his passionate commitment to Buddhism. Singularly admirable is his frank admission that

Buddhism continues to fail with me. It fails with everybody because we're still ego-centric pains. I'm still self-seeking, still have problems, still get unhappy sometimes, still have worries. So it continues to fail, which means that it's not at fault, but that I continue not to use it well enough.[5]

Thurman's honesty is free from all anxiety. He watches, with classic Buddhist detachment, his own failure, beholding it from a distance. He knows that he must strive more diligently to stay on course, that his success in finding happiness is not guaranteed, and that failure, inevitable though it is, must not deter him.

Part III
Transcending Reason

5

Only in Heaven (Christianity)

The belief in a personal god, a belief never held by the ancient Greeks or Romans, initiated a radical change in how Westerners thought about happiness. For those who accepted it, the historical truth of the Christian God, as manifested in both revelation (the Bible) and incarnation (Jesus, the Word made flesh), became the pre-eminent fact of life. One of its consequences was that happiness came to be understood, and exclusively so, as an intimate relationship with God. In the immediate post-classical world, the world of the fourth and fifth centuries AD, the locus of happiness shifted from this life to the next. Only in the afterlife, as Christians have been taught from the earliest times, could anyone enjoy true happiness. This true happiness would outshine any happiness that we could achieve here on earth, just as God outshines man. And yet such happiness cannot be guaranteed because it is unattainable through human effort alone and requires the gift of God's grace.

The Christian idea of a transcendent happiness would have made no sense to Seneca, Marcus Aurelius and all the other Roman Stoics, who believed in a self-wrought happiness that could be forged right here, right now, through sheer willpower. We, too, might think that the Stoics had the better argument, for like them we tend to value self-reliance and individual initiative. Yet for early church fathers like Augustine, roused into battle against pagan cults and philosophies, this was a shocking impiety – on the scale of Prometheus stealing the power of fire from the gods. Let no one, the Bishop of Hippo commanded, believe that through his own unaided effort he might achieve happiness here on earth – *that* was impossible, and merely to conceive it was sinful because it made man God's equal.

Not until the thirteenth century, at the height of its power and influence, did the medieval church allow for a (somewhat) more earth-bound approach to happiness, one that acknowledged a link between the necessarily partial happiness to be obtained in this life and the ultimate felicity to be enjoyed only in heaven. The enlargement of the traditional Christian idea of happiness was the work of two men: a dead pagan philosopher from Athens and a young Dominican friar from southern Italy. The pagan was Aristotle.

'The Dumb Ox'

In the castle of Roccasecca, north of Naples, where he was later imprisoned by his brothers, was born the youngest son of the Conte d'Aquino. History – and heaven – know him as Thomas Aquinas (1224–74), saint of the Roman Catholic Church, author of the *Summa Theologiae* and reconciler of reason and faith. The scion of an aristocratic family (his great uncle, Frederick Barbarossa, had been the Holy Roman Emperor), Aquinas was sent, aged five, to be educated at the Benedictine monastery at nearby Monte Cassino. His father, partly to find a useful career for his quiet but thoughtful seventh son, and partly to make amends for having sided with the Holy Roman Emperor to sack the monastery, proposed that the young Thomas be received as a Benedictine monk. Since worldly rank mattered in a medieval monastery, and especially there, the boy was tapped as a future Abbot of Monte Cassino. All problems resolved.

And then it fell apart. Aquinas went on to study at the University of Naples, where he came under the enlightened influence of the Dominicans, a new order of mendicant preachers, and then among the few people in Christendom to have read the newly translated works of Aristotle. (We shall come back to Aristotle's influence, for it explains much of what Aquinas believed about happiness.) His head stuffed with radical new ideas, Aquinas promptly returned to the family castle and told his father that instead of becoming the feudal lord of a monastery he would spurn the trappings of nobility and beg for his food as a poor friar. The news did not go down well.

Family honour was at stake, and the turncoat Thomas had to be turned back again. His brothers kidnapped him and for a year held him prisoner at Roccasecca, as if he were no better than a serf who had stolen a mule. But Aquinas, not yet twenty, had a mule's stubbornness, and he refused to yield. So the brothers tempered their vengeance, and tried to persuade him with earthly delights. One night, as Aquinas slept, they smuggled a beautiful young woman into his chamber in the hope that lust would get the better of him. How despicable their hope was, for they knew that he had already taken a vow of celibacy. What they failed to count on was the strength of that vow. Awaking to the erotic vision, Aquinas leapt out of bed, brandished a flaming torch and chased the poor shrieking woman out of the room. He bolted the door behind her; and then, in a rare display of violent anger, thrust the firebrand into the door, burning into the blackened wood a sign of the cross. His brothers, shamed and defeated, set free their chaste sibling, who left immediately for Paris, where, at last, he entered the order founded by St Dominic.

In Paris, and later Cologne, Aquinas studied with the German theologian Albertus Magnus, better known as Albert the Great. Great because he was unafraid of science and reason, especially when explained by pagan Greek philosophers or Muslim scholars. Among the religious novices who flocked to his lectures was, in G.K. Chesterton's description from his marvellous little biography, 'one student, conspicuous by his tall and bulky figure, and completely failing or refusing to be conspicuous for anything else'.[1] This young man was so silent in classroom debates, and so lumbering in his walk, that his schoolfellows cruelly nicknamed him the Dumb Ox. Yet Aquinas (for it was he) knew more than he let on. Albert knew the humility of genius when he saw it, even if others were blind; and he retorted, prophetically, 'You call him a Dumb Ox; I tell you this Dumb Ox shall bellow so loud that his bellowing will fill the world.'

In 1252, Friar Thomas returned to Paris, where he finished his studies and began his teaching career. In later years he was assigned to Dominican houses in Naples, Orvieto and Rome (as a mendicant friar, he made all these journeys on foot), where he lectured, preached and began to write his unfinished masterpiece the *Summa Theologiae*, 'The Summation of All Theology'. It was in the *Summa* – a work that for centuries has been caricatured, mostly by those who have not read it, as nothing but pedantic distinctions and pointless speculation about angels on pinheads – that Aquinas devoted so much respectful attention to the pursuit of happiness.

For twenty years Aquinas kept up a driving pace of intellectual labour, writing more than forty books (dictating, actually; his hand-written scrawl was indecipherable). But in December 1273, at the Benedictine priory in Naples, where he was working on a treatise on the sacrament of penance for the *Summa*, something extraordinary, and extraordinarily mysterious, happened to him. As he celebrated mass on the morning of the 6th of December, the feast day of St Nicholas, he was struck by some miraculous vision or mystic insight, the details of which Aquinas never shared, not even to his intimate friend and confessor, Friar Reginald of Piperno. From that day forward he never wrote another word, never dictated another sentence to his scribes. As if in a perpetual trance, he devoted himself entirely to prayer. Reginald, puzzled by this behaviour (the friars joked that Aquinas dictated theological treatises in his sleep), implored him to return to his great unfinished work. Wearily, and impatiently, too, Thomas replied, 'After what I have seen, all that I have written seems like straw to me.'

Why this prodigious scholar, not yet fifty, so abruptly abandoned his life's work remains a mystery. Did he fall ill? Did he succumb to nervous exhaustion? Perhaps he suffered brain damage from a stroke – the other friars observed that he had difficulty speaking and walking and seemed constantly dazed (*stupefactus*). The miracle-seeking hagiographers who wrote the earliest biographies of Aquinas attributed the overnight change to a mystical experience in which he realised the essential futility of expressing the divine in human terms.

Whatever its cause, the sudden renunciation was an ill omen: within three months he was dead. Early in the new year, he had been called by Pope Gregory X to attend the Second Council of Lyons. At the beginning of February he and Friar Reginald set out and headed north for France. They had been travelling only a few days when Thomas struck his head against a tree branch that hung over the road. The injury proved to be fatal, and on the morning of the 7th of March 1274, lying in the guesthouse of the Cistercian abbey at Fossanova, south of Rome, Thomas Aquinas entered history as the greatest mind that Christianity had known in nearly a thousand years.

Learning from the pagans

When the invading armies of Alaric sacked Rome in AD 410, the lamp of Western civilisation, if not exactly extinguished, was turned down to a flicker. Eight hundred years would pass before the works of Aristotle, the common currency of educated Greeks and Romans, resurfaced in the Christian West. For nearly a millennium, the Islamic world, stretching from India to Spain, preserved the heritage of classical antiquity. It was this heritage that Europe coveted, and eventually reclaimed for itself. Yet it was the great Muslim intellectuals Ibn Sina (Avicenna) (980–1037) and Ibn Rushd (Averroes) (1126–98) who translated and wrote commentaries on Greek and Latin texts when Europe was still imprisoned in the proverbial Dark Ages. It was an irony of the time that while Christian crusaders in the Middle East were intent on demolishing Islam, Muslims in Spain were shoring up the West's intellectual foundation.

Beginning in the thirteenth century, the writings of Aristotle, and learned essays upon them, appeared in southern Europe in Latin translations of Arabic versions and the original Greek texts. The Latin texts were sent to monasteries and to the handful of universities – Paris, Toulouse, Bologna, Cologne, Oxford and Cambridge – then in their infancy. (Medieval universities were themselves religious institutions, for the Pope often granted their charters, and theology was one of their principal subjects.) It is sobering to remember that Aristotle was twice as remote to the Middle Ages as the Middle Ages is to us. While more than seven hundred years separate us from Aquinas, fifteen hundred distanced him from the pagan philosopher. To someone in the Middle Ages, classical antiquity was a remote civilisation, more remote than it seems to us today.

For medieval Christianity, the rediscovery of classical thought was not an entertaining prospect but a pernicious threat that shook the Church to its core. Suddenly, and without welcome, here was a body of knowledge, a way of understanding the world, which had been hidden for centuries. Hidden, that is, from European Christians, for whom Aristotle's treatises tackling the biggest of the big questions – ethics, politics, science and metaphysics – came as a disturbing revelation. They were sweeping in scope, persuasive in rationality and untouched by Christian doctrine. At times they contradicted it, and thus gave licence to the heresy that revealed biblical truth – the word of God spoken through his prophets – was not the only truth on offer. To study a pagan philosopher whose ideas threatened the very basis of Christian belief was, to put it mildly, a risky business.

As risk-averse as any multinational organisation, the medieval Church, in the person of the Archbishop of Paris, banned outright every single word that Aristotle had written. But thought crimes continued to be perpetrated, and nowhere more successfully, or more creatively, than among ecclesiastics themselves, who stole into the *scriptoria* of monasteries across Europe to read Aristotle's intellectual pornography.

Over time, however, the Church adopted a shrewdly accommodating stance, recognising the strategic benefit of using Greek philosophy to elaborate Christian doctrine. For a rising generation of scholastics, the new challenge was not to censor Aristotle, but to refute whatever in his writings contradicted biblical revelation, to retain whatever was consistent with Church teaching, and, above all, to emulate the philosopher's rigorous analytical method. The approach sounds iniquitous, but its goal was a generous one: to prove that there was no fundamental conflict between Christian theology and Greek philosophy; nothing incompatible between faith and reason.

Known as the 'Great Synthesis', this heroic intellectual project was begun in Paris by Albert the Great and completed in Naples by his prize pupil, Thomas Aquinas, the bellowing dumb ox. It is a cliché among theologians (and an offence among classicists) to say that Aquinas baptised Aristotle. A less exaggerated appraisal might be that he made the Christian world safe for Aristotle's rational and pragmatic way of thinking – especially about things like happiness. For no one has been more responsible than the humble Dominican friar, undaunted as he was by judgemental traditionalists, for weaving the logical system of a heathen philosopher into the patterned, if now tattered, cloth of Christianity. Logic, when placed in the right hands, could become a very useful tool for surveying the path to happiness.

Faith and reason

Aristotle, blessed with a sunny Mediterranean outlook, took for granted that the world originated in an eternal goodness and possessed a fundamental order and purpose. More gloomily, Christians believed that the world, although originally created by a good and loving God, was corrupted when that temptress Eve gave to Adam the forbidden fruit. Right from the start, the dilemma for Christians has been whether to emphasise God's goodness or humankind's wickedness.

For Aristotle, the concept of 'original sin' would have made no sense; it was a form of self-punishment, and no rational person, he believed, would choose to punish himself. Aquinas, although not free to ignore the reality of sin, could still accentuate the positive part of the story of Genesis. By keeping the spotlight, as it were, on divine benevolence, he found a way to reflect upon God's unconditional love for us and his wish that we be happy. Indeed, true happiness, as Aquinas understood it, consists in nothing other than the contemplation of God's essence. Although such perfect beatitude cannot be attained in this world, the world has been created so that, by leading a virtuous life, we may prepare ourselves for the ultimate happiness that awaits in heaven. (Though he expressed it mystically, Ghazali believed much the same.) Scarred and disfigured though our sins have made it, the world exists not for our misery but for our joy.

Aquinas never doubted that God *wants* us to find happiness. At the moment of creation, the Creator pointed us in the direction of bliss. Of course, we humans have only two ways of knowing what God wants: faith and reason. It is no secret that many religions have their suspicions about reason, and Christianity has been no exception. As that legendary pessimist Augustine taught, reason – the ability to distinguish between true and false – was fallible and so could become the instrument of pride and deception. Biblical revelation and Church doctrine, so he preached, were the sole guides to unerring truth. Aquinas took much from Augustine, but he did not take it hook, line and sinker. He was not willing to declare that faith and reason were in conflict. Just the opposite: they were in harmony (although at times the harmony was tuned to a pitch beyond our hearing), and the lowliest fact could lead us to the highest truth.

There must have been something of the Neapolitan peasant in Aquinas, for he was commonsensical enough to believe that God gave us a mind so that we would use it, and seek to know the nature and cause of all things, including himself. But reason is reasonable enough to know its limits. (Only the deluded man believes his powers are boundless.) On reason's wings, we fly high; but not so high that we touch the face of God, for the finite cannot know the infinite. As

Aquinas put it, a mere 'created substance' cannot know a 'divine essence'.[2] So our natural desire to know absolutely everything can be fully, completely and lastingly satisfied only through revelation, which is how God unveils his identity to mankind. Yet revelation is not the adversary of reason but its fulfilment and perfection. Reason, although necessarily limited, composes a wisdom and does not ensnare us in delusion's trap. Reason is how we enter into God's plan for our happiness; how we know what happiness means.

This, if nothing else, tells us why the 'Dark Ages' are so appallingly misnamed. Though the lesson was lost in later times (and is still lost for some), the medieval Church declared that there can be no ultimate contradiction between what reason tells us and faith gives us. Those two lamps of knowledge shine each upon the other. In our moment of globally resurgent religious fundamentalism, the thirteenth century suddenly, and to our shame, appears more modern than the twenty-first.

The magnetic pull of truth

Nowhere is the perfection of reason through faith more evident than in the *Summa Theologiae*, the monumental work that Aquinas began in 1265 – and then refused to finish because of his own inner or mystical experience. Incomplete though it is, the *Summa* stands as the foremost example of medieval 'scholastic' theology, which means that its goal is not to explain this or that biblical passage but to organise the totality of revelation into a logical and systematic whole. The *Summa* is an enormous magnet that draws in the many disparate truths that God has revealed to mankind throughout history, finding unity where there seems only diversity.

For all its high intellectual ambition, Aquinas wrote the work *ad eruditionem incipientium*: for the instruction of beginners, as he states several times in the preface. A devoted teacher, Aquinas was thinking of his students and their need not for hair-splitting scholarship but for a grand overview of the logical coherence of divinely revealed truth. He had the gift of all great teachers, which was first to immerse himself in deep learning and then to condense that learning so that it could be grasped in its totality by even the densest pupil. And yet it is precisely the astounding scope and measured pace of Aquinas's work that will frustrate modern readers, accustomed as we are to absorbing knowledge rapidly and in bits and pieces, through soundbites, slogans and headlines. The merest glimpse of a single page from the *Summa* will reveal it to be tightly structured, dauntingly dense and altogether lacking in warmth and charm.

Each of the *Summa*'s three long parts is divided into formally stated questions on distinctive topics, such as 'Does happiness consist in earthly goods?'. Each question, in turn, is sub-divided into articles that examine particular issues within the stated topic, such as 'whether wealth is necessary for happiness' (wealth being one of the 'earthly goods' under discussion). To answer the several queries posed in each article, Aquinas follows a fixed method: he lists, as precisely as possible, the objections to his own view; he makes his case, quoting relevant theological and philosophical texts; and, finally, he refutes each of the objections that he had so carefully stated at the outset.

The *Summa* contains 613 questions divided into 3,125 articles, with nearly 10,000 objections and refutations. Each article, which really has the character of a conversation or dialogue, begins with the interrogative *ultrum* ('whether') – that one word signalling that the matter is not settled in advance, but is that rare thing: a genuinely open question. The answers offered (and there are thousands of them) are not fixed or final but provisional and subject to future discussion and debate. Provisional not because truth is arbitrary but because it is mysterious and many-sided. In its spirit of discovery and dialogue, the *Summa* feels surprisingly, but reassuringly, modern.

What seems alien to us, though, is its precision and formality; there is nothing casual about Aquinas's prose. But that is exactly what his original readers would have expected. In its structure, the *Summa* derives entirely from the medieval *disputatio*, the highly ritualised classroom debates conducted by eagerly adversarial religious novices. Aquinas stuck to this approach for the sensible reason that he knew it best, having mastered it while studying with Albert the Great in Paris and Cologne. We need to picture the young Aquinas partici, pating in these academic games – hesitantly, though; he was still the 'dumb ox' – alongside scores of other young men who, although more combative, were less clever.

How might this remnant of a long-vanished moment speak to us today, particularly to those of us who stand apart from its untroubled presumption of religious belief? In our time of abrasive journalism and political debates that quickly descend into juvenile retorts, it is easy to miss what is (for us) most unusual about how Aquinas argued his points: that he fought not *against* his opponent but *for* the truth. That is why he began every argument by stating his opponent's view not in the weakest but the strongest terms. Indeed, he starts not as the aggressive questioner but as the patient listener; with good will, he tries to reckon with the position of those who disagree with him. Only that way will an argument be convincingly overthrown: not by the witty phrase or the rhetorical turn; still less by name calling and fist thumping. For Aquinas, an intellectual dispute was no jousting match, in which competitors tried to unseat one another, but a common search for truth. Truth as it could be demonstrated – to everyone – by the light and guidance of reason.

The truth, as Aquinas believed it, about happiness is found in the second part of the *Summa*, where he discusses human action. The Latin term for happiness, and the one that Aquinas uses throughout, is *beatitudo*. For Christians, especially, the word immediately calls to mind the Sermon on the Mount, when Jesus spoke the beatitudes: 'Blessed are the meek', 'Blessed are the poor', and so on. (We might think of that famous sermon as a public preaching on happiness, something akin to a Christian version of Buddha's sermon in the deer park at Benares.) What is contained in the word *beatitudo* is precisely this sense of 'blessedness': not simply a higher or better state of being, but one that is closer to God, warmed by his radiance. This sense of drawing near to God is the core of Aquinas's vision of happiness, and one that today we might find confusing, irrelevant or even offensive. But, generous interlocutor that he is, Aquinas anticipated our doubts. He tries to persuade us through reason, and reason alone, that perfect happiness exists only in heaven, in the contemplation of God's essence. Those who know their catechism will recognise this as the 'beatific vision'.

Aquinas puts his case in five questions about happiness, which are known collectively as *De vita beata* ('Treatise on Happiness'). Only within the last fifty years has an English version become available in anything other than one of the few translations of the entire *Summa*. For nearly seven centuries, then, it was mainly theologians and their students (who could read the original Latin text) who knew firsthand of Aquinas's belief that happiness

- is the ultimate end of human life (Question 1)
- does not consist in earthly goods (Question 2)
- consists only in the vision of God (Question 3)
- has requirements (Question 4)
- is possible only in heaven (Question 5)

Happiness, the final frontier

Aquinas presumes that mankind is naturally curious, and thus shares Aristotle's conviction, expressed in the opening sentence of his *Metaphysics*, that '[a]ll human beings by nature desire to know'. To know, however, is not merely to gather up information but to seek out origins and uncover causes. (Example: to know why objects of unequal weight fall at the same speed is to uncover the law of gravity.) Although it appears forward moving and progressive, knowledge is actually a working back towards first principles. We gaze with wonderment upon the world and are moved to know who created it, and why. It was no innocent thing for Aquinas to believe that man is naturally curious, for such a belief declares that knowledge could *never* be a forbidden fruit.

One thing that mankind can know is itself; we can seek to discover the purpose and meaning of *our* existence. As good rationalists, we begin that voyage of discovery with the guiding principle that each living thing has a distinctive purpose or state of completion towards which it naturally tends. This state of completion, which Aquinas called 'specific perfection' (a concept he learned from Aristotle), varies from creature to creature according to its distinctive capabilities: seeds grow into fruit-bearing plants, caterpillars become butterflies, frolicking colts become tamed horses and impetuous children mature into rational adults. By 'perfection', Aquinas does not mean flawlessness but rather the complete attainment of what a thing is supposed to be. (When someone says they are 'perfectly satisfied', they mean that they are completely so.) Mankind is unique among all living things because it enlists reason to seek its perfection. We act deliberately to move ever closer to the fulfilment of our natural purpose, thus becoming most truly ourselves.

In Aquinas's discussion of happiness, the starting point is that whenever we act, we act for a purpose: 'each thing desires its own fulfilment and therefore desires for its ultimate end a good that perfects and completes it'.[3] Just as we climb a staircase to reach the top, we undertake action to achieve a certain outcome. In that sense, all human actions, provided they are guided by reason, are purposeful movements towards intended goals. (Involuntary mechanisms, such as blinking, sneezing and growing older, are the exceptions.) These goals are neither scattered nor isolated, but arranged in a hierarchy. We work to earn money; we earn money to pay our mortgage; we pay our mortgage to have a secure home; we have a secure home to provide for our family. And so on. But where does it end? Is there a last link in the chain of goals?

Aquinas was certain, as was Aristotle, that there *must* be a final goal to guide our every action and to impose coherence on the chaos of life. Instead of contending with an infinite series of purposes, inevitably in conflict, we need to stay focused on the supreme, governing one. Just as a train makes intermediary stops but has only one terminus, we have intermediary goals but only one final end. Whatever we do and whatever we desire, we do and desire it for the sake of this ultimate goal. If we lacked such a final purpose, we would never experience any moment of accomplishment, for there would be nothing to accomplish. It would be like shooting arrows without a target: we would never hit the mark because it would not be there to be hit.

But what *is* this target that we all aim at? What is this single point of destination towards which we are all headed? It is nothing other than happiness. This is no mere greeting-card pleasantry. For when Aquinas asserts that eternal beatitude – everlasting happiness – is the true end of human life, he does not mean anything so trivial as happiness is a nice thing to have and we should do all we can to find it. No, his meaning is far more urgent: that happiness is our complete and perfect good; that God created us to be happy; that our desire to be happy is natural. And just as it is unnatural for a plant to turn away from the sun, it is unnatural for mankind to turn away from happiness.

Our heart's desire

For Aquinas, the only definition of happiness that can be logically defended is the perfect happiness that consists in the vision of God in heaven. As the supreme object of desire, God overrides, indeed obliterates, all lesser desires. This, Aquinas would argue, stands to reason: since we desire things in proportion to their goodness, we desire God most of all because he alone is infinite goodness. But some of us are standing in reason's shadow, not its light. We are trapped by inferior versions of happiness, mistakenly believing that a 'created good' – anything that exists in the world or is part of our own being – can make us truly happy.

Aquinas, like so many of the world's great thinkers about the good life, whether Epicurus, the Stoics or Buddha, believes that no worldly possession – wealth, honour, power or glory – can be the source of happiness. Wealth, whether money or the things that money can buy, is always sought for the sake of something else; at the most basic level, food, clothing and shelter. To desire one thing for the sake of another is to desire it as the means to an end but not as the end itself. Since happiness is the *ultimate* end, its source cannot be wealth. Nor can we equate happiness with honour, because honour is not a character trait but the deference shown by one person to another. Honour recognises excellence, but is not excellence itself. Still less can happiness reside in glory, since glory is nothing but public praise, and yet praise can be unmerited. (The modern word for false glory is 'celebrity'.) That would make happiness the product of imperfect human knowledge, and thus prone to error. Finally, happiness cannot be found in power, because while happiness is a perfect good, power can be used for evil.

Nor should we make the mistake of assuming that happiness is an internal good, as if the perfection of the body (the whitest teeth, the smoothest skin) were somehow morally superior to the pursuit of worldly goods. As Aquinas explains, everywhere we look nature tells us that happiness does not consist in bodily perfection, whether superior strength, robust health or exceptional longevity. Man is happier than any animal, yet deer are faster, lions stronger and tortoises older. Moreover, the goods of the body serve only to preserve life and do not aim at anything greater. That puts them at odds with the view of happiness as a goal, because goals imply movement towards a destination. Anyone who claims that their goal is self-preservation is as ludicrous as a marathon runner who thinks he can win by running in place. What matters is moving towards the finishing line. In a final objection, Aquinas observes that bodily pleasures include the senses, but exclude the intellect, which is the highest human faculty. Since happiness, in order to *be* happiness, must be perfect and complete, it cannot be limited to anything so partial as sensuous pleasures.

Aquinas would say that while we are meant to enjoy worldly goods and goods of the body, we do wrong to mistake that enjoyment for true happiness. Of course the millionaire rejoices in his wealth, the diplomat in her reputation, the film star in fame, the runway model in beauty, the Olympian in strength and the Nobel laureate in genius. But only a limited, and thus unsatisfying, happiness can be derived from those attributes, because they are passing, not permanent. Even if someone were amazingly rich, highly esteemed, globally famous, stunningly gorgeous, fearsomely strong and prodigiously intelligent, it would not be enough. The happiness of the world's most fortunate person would still be undermined by the feeling – the fear – that something could go wrong. The only time nothing will go wrong, the only time all our desires will be satisfied, Aquinas reminds us, is when we make God himself the consummation of all desire.

Deep (and high) thoughts

Unlike God, who is happy in his own essence, mankind must search for and achieve its happiness. For Aquinas, that achievement was a union with God, a sharing or participating in the divine uncreated good. Here, again, we glimpse the shadow of Aristotle, who also insisted that happiness was an activity: a purposeful movement towards fulfilment. By 'activity', Aquinas had in mind a rather particular kind of effort. He did not mean mere motion, such as walking or running, or acting upon an object, such as chopping wood. Nor did he mean a preference for worldly affairs, for living what we commonly call an 'active life'.

Activity is something truly dynamic: the progression from potentiality to actuality, immaturity to maturity and imperfection to perfection. When we say that the time is 'ripe', or that a friend, previously shy and retiring, has suddenly 'blossomed', we are getting close to the *developmental* sense of activity that for Aquinas was so important. The thing to be developed most of all is life itself. Our life shouldn't just ramble along – one damn thing after another – but should move purposefully towards a final, fulfilling goal.

For Aquinas, the supreme activity of life is the search for happiness, and it is conducted through the intellect. This much stands to reason: because happiness is man's highest end, its attainment must rely upon man's highest faculty, which is the intellect. (Though followers of St Francis of Assisi would argue that love is man's highest faculty.) But the part of the intellect that really interests Aquinas is contemplation, which he regards as the highest function of mankind's highest faculty. In other words, contemplation is the single greatest activity that we can undertake.

To be happy we must contemplate, but we cannot contemplate just anything: a daisy, a Calvin Klein model or the second law of thermodynamics. Since happiness is our highest end, we must use our intellect to contemplate the highest object, the most final and absolute thing that can be known. Only one entity, Aquinas believes, meets that criterion: God, the architect and governor of the universe. The happiness we derive from contemplating him will be perfect (and cannot be anything *other* than perfect) because God, the first cause of everything, is perfection itself. Only in this 'vision of the divine essence', Aquinas declares, can we attain 'ultimate and perfect happiness'.[4]

Face to face

Like Ghazali before him, Aquinas believed that the highest form of happiness was a direct encounter with God and the pleasure that arises from beholding his face. But only in heaven shall we gaze upon the beatific vision, and see God face to face. According to the Christian view, true happiness is transcendent and supernatural. In mortal life we can achieve, at best, only a partial and incomplete happiness. Like other religions, Christianity offers a powerful rebuke to the seeming appeal of earthly fortunes and worldly goods: they fail to merit our exclusive attention because they fail to make us supremely happy.

Augustine pessimistically believed that no happiness was possible in this life except for the mere hope of happiness in the next. (If you were a Roman, and the barbarians were at the gate, you might think the same thing, too.) But Aquinas inclined towards the more balanced view that in this life we can be allotted a share of the plenitude of happiness that waits in heaven. In a cheerier mood, he explained that humanity can indeed participate in celestial happiness (*participatio beatitudinis*).

Even so, Aquinas's perspective is asymmetric. Happiness in our lifetime must always fall short of perfect happiness in heaven because the divine essence (the contemplation of which *is* happiness) remains hidden to us here on earth. Agonisingly, we feel that some part of God remains inaccessible, and we suffer in our painful awareness that as long as the beatific vision is eclipsed we cannot know true happiness. God's true nature must, for now, remain a mystery to the human mind, since 'all that man knows of God is to know that he does not know him'.[5]

The frustration we feel at being separated from God is no mere annoyance, like failing to complete a crossword puzzle. It is, rather, a profound feeling of helplessness: we were made to know God (Aquinas never doubted that) and yet we cannot know him; we cannot achieve our own destiny. We search the world for God, but never do we find him. At best, we see only his trace, his fingerprint. The miracle of birth is a sign that God created us; the laws of nature reveal his genius; the thunder roars his potency; and the distant stars shine with his infinity. As the poet Gerard Manley Hopkins rhap-sodised, 'The world is charged with the grandeur of God.' But the world is not charged with God himself. Of him we know nothing – and yet upon him our happiness depends entirely.

So we are left with the unsettling and yet optimistic belief that to be happy, completely and everlastingly happy, we must behold the divine essence that is nowhere found on earth. The New Testament writers assure us that what we will find in heaven is no mere reflection or image of God (such as we encounter in the world) but an actual vision of his pure being. As St Paul famously told the Christians of Corinth: 'For now we see through a glass, darkly; but then face to face.' What the Damascene convert meant was that, once apprehended, the beatific vision gives us clear, immediate and direct knowledge of God, far beyond the shadowy knowledge available to us here on earth, where we must approach divinity indirectly, through symbols, signs and allegories. The brilliance of the vision will never fade, Aquinas contends, for 'the mind of man will be united to God in one, continual, everlasting activity'.[6]

Amazingly, grace

Striving, in this life, through reason and virtue, we can attain only a hint of the complete and everlasting beatitude that awaits us in the hereafter. Incapable as we are of becoming perfectly happy through our own resources, we rely on God's help. As we stand on the threshold of celestial bliss, unable to cross over, God comes to our rescue. He raises us up through the gift of his grace.

Like all gifts, grace is unmerited. Aquinas is perfectly clear about that. God freely gives his grace to a sinful, undeserving humanity, a humanity that cannot earn the gift, but only accept it. We desire to know God because God himself instilled the desire in our hearts from the first moment of creation. God made us to be reunited with him, and it would be a perverse God who denied his creation the possibility of satisfying that desire. Grace is what makes the possibility possible.

But the gift of grace does not absolve us of responsibility, as if we could just lie around waiting for grace to drop out of the sky and be showered upon us. No, we must meet grace halfway, Aquinas insists. We must do our bit, make our own effort to be virtuous. For virtue, the foundation of imperfect, earthly happiness, will orient us towards perfect, celestial happiness. What Aquinas has in mind are the traditional Aristotelian moral virtues of justice, courage, temperance and prudence, along with the classically Christian virtues (Aquinas calls them 'theological virtues' because they flow from God) of faith, hope and charity. They are the habit, or disposition, to do the right thing. Through God's grace we take the final step on the path to eternal happiness; but just to put ourselves on that path we must act virtuously. In the pursuit of happiness, virtue is the minimum requirement. We are gravely mistaken to believe that in this life we can commit acts of malice and atrocity, and then, suddenly, through divine grace, find ourselves transported into the realm of eternal bliss. That would make a mockery of morality.

The thundering silence of St Thomas

The exquisite irony of the life of Thomas Aquinas is that the last message of this man so driven to express himself in the steady drumbeat of words was ... silence. Silent not because he had nothing more to say, but because there was no way of saying it. Aquinas had reached down to the deep inexpressible mystery of things, and touched upon a truth that words fail utterly to convey. This silence, which not even his devoted sister could break, nor his dearest companion, Friar Reginald, lasted to the moment of his death.

The great *Summa* was left unfinished not because death stayed the author's hand, but because the author had lived long enough – no, profoundly enough – to realise that the works of the hand can never express the wonders of the heart. Like other theologians of his time, Aquinas had learned about a wise Persian mystic from an earlier century, named 'Algazal'. Perhaps when his own mystic vision descended upon him, the Christian monk gained a deeper appreciation for the Islamic scholar's conviction that silence, just as much as words, could express the truth.

What the vision must have brought home to Aquinas was that the true essence of things is unfathomable, and in the last resort reason cannot find it. No answers we can give will ever be sufficient for the questions we want to ask. And yet there is a way to know the things that the mind cannot grasp. This way has nothing to do with reason and logic, but everything to do with the transcending of it. Our response to the limitations of reason, to the boundaries of the human mind, cannot be to forsake reason, for that would be only to drown in the deep swirl of ignorance. What is required is something *other* than reason. For want of a better word, we may call it imagination, although it has been called other things over the centuries: mystic ecstasy, meditation or simply prayer. Of course we need reason to lead us to imagination, just as we need a boat to travel across the water. But once we have reached the shore, we must get out of the boat to travel further inland. In the same way, reason will have served its purpose when it is 'used up' and we have no choice but to leap beyond it.

Aquinas made just this sort of transcendent leap, or rather it came upon him, in the vision that struck him dumb while he celebrated mass on a cold December morning in 1273. We are drawn back to the story of the final days of Thomas Aquinas because it tells us, more clearly than we can tell ourselves, that there is a sanctity to life that reason cannot touch. And this is his story's lasting lesson: what we know through reason is true, but never enough. That is not a sad lesson, but one of unimaginable joy. We must think of the poor begging friar not as burdened by feelings of despair but uplifted by a surging wave of contentedness and peace. We must imagine him to be happy.

In a way that not even he, the most articulate of men, could express, Aquinas had broken through to an experience of a reality that was unfathomable. Merely thinking of his experience must move us, as it moved him, to silence. The time for books, the reading and the writing of them, must come to an end. But the silence that falls over us will not be one of defeat or despair. It will be a silence of victory. Not triumphant, not boastful, but a quiet thanksgiving for having reached journey's end and seen into the invisible heart of all things.

Bound for heaven

It is no fair criticism of Christianity that not everyone is Christian, just as it is no fair criticism of any faith that not all people profess it. Yet since enlightenment, not religious conversion, is the goal of our inquiry, we can evaluate what Aquinas has to say about happiness quite apart from any requirement of faith or belief. Not everything he says will rise or fall by the truth of Christianity. If Aquinas could hear the voice of truth in Aristotle, perhaps we can hear the same in him.

But what we hear may not be to our liking. The note struck repeatedly throughout Aquinas's writings, and for us it is likely to be clanging and discordant, is that perfect happiness is unattainable in this life. Such a refrain we hear again and again, and never in the quietest tones. This is a too exalted view of happiness, one that does not sit comfortably with our modern belief in self-sufficiency. Why would God create us with the desire to contemplate his essence – the desire hard-wired in our brain, like that for food and drink – and yet deny us the means to satisfy it?

Heavenly happiness may well be, and certainly Aquinas believes it to be, the enhanced continuation of earthly happiness. But there is no guarantee that we will end up in heaven. We do not know whether perfect happiness awaits us, nor can we calculate our chances of attaining it because that very attainment lies beyond mortal power. Christianity does provide, through God's grace, the means to achieve perfect happiness, a glimpse of which we can catch here on earth in the kind of breakthrough moment that Aquinas himself experienced. But since we cannot earn or merit grace, we simply have to trust that God will freely and unfailingly bestow it upon us. Surely this is a disdainful view of human life: we can neither renounce our desire for happiness nor requite it.

And yet to end so discouragingly would be to render falsely Aquinas's vision of happiness. For as much as he insisted on the need for divine grace, and as much as he counselled that reason, however exalted, must be exceeded, he never lost sight of the truth that our search for happiness begins, and must begin, in the practicalities of life. If happiness is an accomplishment, and Aquinas held that it was, then where else would we start to accomplish it than here on earth?

Of all the lessons that the Catholic saint learned from the pagan Greek philosopher, maybe the most surprising one (surprising because *we* have tended to forget it) is that what is most authentic about mankind is the union of body and soul. Aquinas, in a way that defies all subsequent caricature, did not regard the body as the root of all evil, the locus of shame. Christ himself was the Word made *flesh*. On his deathbed, Aquinas (himself a sometime poet) called for the Song of Solomon to be read to him. At the moment he was about to relinquish his body he wanted nothing so much as to hear a love poem, and thus be reminded of the body's delights. There can be no surer sign than this that mankind's supreme happiness, although it must transcend the world, can never renounce it. The path to happiness may well take us deep into a mystery whose resolution lies in a sphere beyond our immediate reach, but that path is open to all, even to the dumbest ox.

6

The Alchemy of Happiness
(Islam)

An Islamic tradition (*hadith*) states that at the start of every century God sends someone to revitalise and inspire the community of the faithful. The great reformer of the fifth century of the Islamic era was Abu Hamid al-Ghazali (1058–1111), 'The Proof of Islam', 'The Ornament of Faith' and 'The Renewer of Religion'. Ghazali believed that God had called him to renew Islam in its moment of crisis, and for many Muslims his authority is second only to that of the prophet Muhammad. He must be counted as one of the most original spiritual thinkers of any culture in any age.

Born in the Persian city of Tûs, in the northeast province of Khorasan, Ghazali demonstrated an early passion for knowledge. 'To thirst after a comprehension of things as they really are,' he recalled in his spiritual autobiography, *The Deliverance from Evil*, 'was my habit and custom from a very early age.'[1] An encounter with thieves showed the force of that habit, for he demanded that they return neither his money nor his clothes but only his notebooks. Struck by the boy's audacity – or perhaps just recognising the limited resale value of a student's scribbling – the thieves handed them over. (On the shrewd presumption that such an appeal was unlikely to elicit a similarly enlightened response from other highwaymen, Ghazali spent the next three years memorising the contents of those recovered books.) The story is almost certainly fabricated, but it does make the point that

Ghazali was someone who desired to know everything. The problem, as he himself soon discovered, was that he was going about it the wrong way.

As a young man he went on to study law and theology at the Nizamiyya college in Nishapur, where his talents destined him for an academic career. In 1091, aged only thirty-three, he was appointed professor of law at the Nizamiyya college in Baghdad, one of a number of advanced schools established by Nizam al-Mulk, the vizier of the Turkish sultan, to promote Sunni (orthodox) Islam. Ghazali was now a man of high mark and repute.

Shortly after reaching this position of intellectual eminence, he fell victim, as we know, to a debilitating spiritual crisis. Although never for a moment doubting his faith, Ghazali wondered, nonetheless, whether the lamp of reason could illuminate it. In a way that anticipated Thomas Aquinas, Ghazali believed that reason and faith were partners in the search for ultimate and final truth. So he resolved to search for knowledge beyond doubt and truth beyond corruption. He sought a rational certainty so strong, so steadfast, that not even miracles – the suspension of reason – could overthrow it. But as he found out, the rational mind alone cannot uncover the ultimate truth of things; for there are truths the mind can scarcely imagine, let alone apprehend.

It was during his spiritual crisis that Ghazali became acquainted with Sufism, the mystical side of Islam. Mystics were men not of theories and abstractions, nor of traditions and customs; they were, rather, men of pure experience. And they proved to be a model for Ghazali in his moment of crisis:

> I apprehended clearly that the mystics were men who had real experiences, not men of words, and that I had already progressed as far as was possible by way of intellectual apprehension. What remained for me was not to be attained by oral instruction and study but only by immediate experience and by walking in the mystic way.[2]

Setting out on this road to happiness, Ghazali examined his own life. Although his faith in God was sincere, he was ashamed of his attachment to worldly success, his pride and his hunger for public recognition and esteem. For a time, he lived in fear and indecision. He would awake with a clear resolve to leave Baghdad and forsake his profession, yet by nightfall the morning's confidence had vanished; his faith beckoned him to seek a new life, but the chains of worldly desire held him back. Ghazali could not bring himself to heed the cry of the voice – his own inner voice – that called out to him:

> To the road! To the road! What is left of life is but little and the journey before you is long … If you do not prepare *now* for eternal life, when will you prepare? If you do not now sever these attachments, when will you sever them?[3]

The more Ghazali resisted the call, the more agonising his crisis became. He lost the power of speech, and so was forced to stop teaching. Later, his throat constricted so tightly that he was unable to swallow food. He understood, in a thunderbolt of mystic intuition, that his physical suffering was but the outward sign of an inward sickness. He was sick at heart. In his broken and exhausted state, Ghazali finally accepted that only God could heal him.

So, at the height of his fame, he renounced everything that he had struggled so hard to acquire. Ghazali told his friends that he was making a pilgrimage to Mecca, but that was just a diversionary tactic; he was actually going to Syria and wanted to make the journey alone. Before leaving, Ghazali entrusted his children to the care of close relatives, set aside money for their education, and then gave away his remaining wealth. In his heart he vowed to live the life of a poor Sufi mystic, intent on purging his soul of vices, adorning it with virtue and, ultimately, losing himself in the loving contemplation of God.

When Ghazali left Baghdad, he is said to have taken two mules, both laden with books. Shortly after beginning his journey, robbers sprang upon him. This time, Ghazali was not so persuasive: the thieves overpowered him and made off with every last book. Some years later, in Mecca, after he had experienced an inner awakening, the immortal Sufi guide Khidr appeared to him in a vision. He told Ghazali that if the books had *not* been stolen he would have remained enslaved to them, and so would never have read the 'book' of true knowledge within his heart. Khidr provided the mystic interpretation of the event, revealing the deeper truth under the surface of mere circumstance. No doubt the tales of Ghazali and the book thieves are apocryphal (like so many anecdotes in Sufi texts) for their primary purpose is symbolic: to reveal a hidden meaning. Through the two parallel stories we learn that there is a time to follow the path of reason and a time to depart from it. Wisdom lies in knowing when the time has come to leave reason behind.

Without his books, but with more wisdom, Ghazali settled in Damascus, where he spent two peaceful years in reflection and religious devotion. In the streets and marketplaces of Damascus it would have been difficult for someone of Ghazali's stature to remain completely anonymous, so he must have welcomed the chance to pass his days in undisturbed solitude. He put that solitude to good use, for through the habit of meditation he recovered from his spiritual crisis. The recovery came not through his own power but through (to use his favourite metaphor) the light of God shining into his heart. God's pure gift to a sinful mankind, this light penetrates our soul and pierces our heart with such force that, as Ghazali taught, we have no choice but to renounce this world of illusion and turn our entire being towards the one true reality that is God.

After achieving this state of enlightenment, Ghazali returned himself to the world. He travelled first to Jerusalem, where he prayed at the Dome of the Rock – the site of Solomon's temple and, according to tradition, Abraham's sacrifice of his son Isaac and Muhammad's miraculous night journey to heaven. Ghazali then embarked on a pilgrimage to Mecca – thus fulfilling one of the requirements of traditional Islamic law (the *Sharia*) – a trip which also allowed him to pray at the tombs of Abraham in Hebron and Muhammad in Medina. Only after visiting Mecca did he return to Baghdad, where he was reunited with his children. He eventually moved back to Tûs, his birthplace, where he founded a monastic religious community.

What Ghazali learned in his period of solitude he recorded in his greatest work, *The Revival of the Religious Sciences* (*Ihya 'Ulum ad-Din*), which runs to 6,000 pages across four massive volumes. (It was publicly burned in Muslim Spain before Ghazali became a great religious authority.) Later, he prepared a greatly condensed version of his Arabic masterpiece for the benefit of common readers, who needed spiritual wisdom and moral guidance just as much as the religious elite. Ghazali was careful to write this more popular book in Persian, the vernacular tongue of his countrymen. He called it *The Alchemy of Happiness* (*Kimiya-i-Sa'adat*).

Before long, Ghazali was enticed back into the lecture hall at the Nizamiyya college in Nishapur, where he had studied in his youth. He returned to his profession a changed man:

> I had been disseminating the knowledge by which worldly success is attained … But now I am calling men to the knowledge whereby worldly success is given up and its low position in the scale of real worth is recognised. This is now my intention, my aim, my desire; God knows that this is so. It is my earnest longing that I may make myself and others better. I do not know whether I shall reach my goal or whether I shall be taken away while short of my object.[4]

In one of history's sad ironies, he was taken away from this noble task only a few years later. On the morning of his death, before first light, he asked for a shroud. He kissed it and laid it over his eyes, saying, 'Obediently I enter into the presence of the King.' He stretched out his feet and turned to face Mecca. By sunrise, he was dead.

The journey inward

At the heart of Islam lies the Koran, the sacred text that God revealed to the prophet Muhammad in the cave on Mount Hira around the year 610. The Koran, which embodies the full range of principles and values by which Muslims are called to order their lives, is supplemented by the Prophet's many 'sayings' and reports of his actions and decisions. Together, these texts shape the Muslim tradition known as the 'Prophetic Way' (al-Sunnah). This tradition, like that of the other monotheistic faiths, centres on laws to be obeyed, commandments to be fulfilled and rules to be correctly followed.

Yet the 'religions of the book' have another side, a side that reveals their inner meaning. This further, hidden dimension is mysticism. Not so much a school of thought, mysticism is more an attitude or way of life because it seeks to penetrate through a religion's outward form to find its deeper truth – a truth that cannot be expressed in normal thought and language. Mysticism in all religions has certain shared characteristics. Above all, it is a personal experience, and not a general theory or abstract idea; it requires an inward journey (frequently symbolised as an outward ascent); and it depends not upon logic but upon imagination. In the modern West, mysticism is often misunderstood as self-indulgent, or bundled together with a vague 'New Age' spiritualism, itself a descendant of the 1960s hippie counterculture. All that confusion makes it difficult for us to appreciate the insight and rigour of this ancient and extraordinary spiritual path.

Heirs, as we are, to the rational traditions of science and logic, we might greet with scepticism, perhaps ridicule the mystic's claim that imagination is the path to happiness. But imagination is not alien to reason. (How else do scientific discoveries occur except when scientists *imagine* that something is true – the hypothesis – and then set about to prove it?) Imagination is not about making things up – that is fantasy, which is something entirely different – but about grasping truths that lie beyond our rational comprehension. Through the gateway of imagination, we gain access to what is absent; what is not in view; what is, at least for now, only a possibility. Can we really be surprised that it takes some imagination to be happy? Happiness must, to some extent, be found in a realm beyond reason because it begins with imagining a future reality: the self that we might become.

And so mysticism requires intense imaginative experiences not for any gratuitous reason, but for the legitimate one that it aims at a truth that cannot be put into mere words. Since, by definition, an infinite god is incommensurate with finite human beings, we cannot know God directly; our sense perceptions and rational thoughts will be of no help. Any argument that the human mind can devise for the existence of God is pointless, because wherever God exists, it is in a realm beyond our mind's comprehension. Whoever God is, he is a being beyond logic, which is why science can neither prove nor disprove his existence. Yet if we cannot think of God, still we can *imagine* him. Through myths, symbols and archetypes, we can touch upon a reality that we cannot fully grasp. True, we create such images with our mind, but we *feel* a deeper dimension within them. We intuit a hidden meaning which reason cannot disclose.

Prescribed rules of conduct, the great mystics of all faiths have always believed, are of only limited value in the search for happiness – or the quest for the ground of all being, or the contemplation of God's essence, to state it more theologically. Indeed, at some point such rules might need to be set aside so that individual mystic experience can take the precedence it deserves. 'The enlightened man', as Ghazali wrote, 'knows, not by hearsay or traditional belief, but by actual experience, what produces wretchedness or happiness in the soul'.[5]

Eastern religions have been the most accepting of mysticism precisely because they are not so caught up in rules and commandments. In walking the mystic way, they have less baggage to leave behind. By contrast, the conforming rituals and traditions of Islam, Christianity and Judaism have always been at odds with openness to the power of personal experience. And yet even there, in such seemingly infertile soil, mysticism has taken root. In the history of

Islam, it was mystic thought – Sufism – that gave exuberance and freedom to a tradition that had come to seem rigid and locked.

Ah, sweet mystery

Sufism holds that Islam has two aspects: outward form and inner spirit. (The name is thought to derive from *suf*, the white woollen robe that Muslim mystics have worn for more than a thousand years, and which is said to have been favoured by the Prophet himself.) It emerged within decades of Muhammad's lifetime as a reaction against unduly literal adherence to the laws and forms of Islamic religious culture. By protesting against an exactitude that threatened to reduce their religion to mere blind obedience to rituals and commandments, the Sufis challenged anyone who had accepted Islamic law in a merely superficial way – the outward form – to discover its deep and rich inner meaning. They did not want to overturn religious law so much as they wanted to enrich the understanding of it.

The distinction that the Sufis made between the outward form of religious ritual and its inward aspect is not a cryptic one, for we all understand the difference between form and content, appearance and substance, exterior and interior. Take the example of the five daily prayers that every Muslim is called upon to recite. These ritual actions possess both a surface form and a deep content. Turning to face Mecca when you pray is the outward sign of turning your heart towards God. Similarly, the requirement to purify the site where you pray is the symbol of purifying your heart.

On a grander scale, the pilgrimage to Mecca represents, in its outward form, travel to the world's holiest site. The inner meaning is that we must travel away from our sins, leaving behind our old self: the real pilgrimage is an inward moral journey. The visible actions of prayer and pilgrimage, far from being mere formalities, are charged with symbolic force and remind us of an invisible meaning; but without that meaning, the actions are hollow and empty. Performing a religious ritual in a mechanical way, without purity of intention, is mere pretence, and so does not help us to move closer to God. It is not enough to do the right thing; we must do it for the right reason and in the right spirit.

Every monotheistic religion struggles with tensions that inevitably arise between those who emphasise outward form and those who search for inner meaning. By Ghazali's day, nearly five hundred years after the revelation of the Koran, Islam was threatened by an ever-widening rift between Sufism and orthodox faith. The Sufis were denounced for placing personal experience above religious law, thus allowing themselves (allegedly) to justify any action, however sinful, by claiming that it was divinely inspired. Traditional theologians, meanwhile, were criticised for draining Islam of its vitality and passion; for reducing it to a dull mechanical compliance with rules. It was Ghazali's mission to reconcile these seemingly opposing forces.

Like the Sufi mystic Abu'l-Qasim al-Junayd (d. 910), in whose footsteps he followed, Ghazali believed that mystical knowledge must have boundaries – and that those boundaries were not arbitrary but firmly set by the Koran and the Traditions. Extreme mysticism would harm the Muslim community by encouraging vanity and the neglect of useful labour. If every farmer gave up farming to pursue mystic ecstasy, Ghazali prudently advised, then no one would be left to keep the world going. Yet he also affirmed the reality (although never himself experiencing it) of the mystical union between God and man. We should imagine Ghazali weaving a mystic thread into the whole cloth of Islam, drawing together and uniting what only appeared to be conflicting ideas and beliefs. (The search for common ground is, of course, how *all* societies, Eastern or Western, ancient or modern, solve their problems.)

Moreover, Ghazali's own life is a living symbol of the Sufi path and its integration of outer form and inner reality. Throughout his youth, and until his spiritual crisis, Ghazali had focused entirely on Islam's outer form: the careful study of its laws and the dutiful observance of its rituals. But after his conversion to Sufism, he gained a mystical insight into the deeper truth that could scarcely be expressed in any outward, material way. During his years of prayerful solitude and wandering, he cultivated this new experience of entering more profoundly, more soulfully, we might say, into prophetic revelation. The culminating moment, the moment of integration, came in the last years of his life when he returned home to teach. As Ghazali was careful to point out, his return to his birthplace was not a simple 'going back' to the way things had been previously, because he himself was now transformed. Because he had been transformed he could guide others to the truth that had been disclosed to him.

Ghazali was particularly struck by the story of Junayd reproaching a novice for shrieking ecstatically while listening to music during a Sufi assembly. After a period of self-imposed restraint, the youth's pent-up emotions were so intense that he uttered one last shriek and died on the spot. In one sense, the story conveys the paradoxical truth (as expressed in the *hadith* 'die before you die') that in life we must die to our false self and be reborn as our true self. This is a fundamental Sufi principle, and we shall soon come back to it. In a cautionary sense, though, the story of the shrieking novice reminds us that extreme outward expressions of mystical understanding can be fraudulent or counterfeit. Irrational behaviour does not, in itself, express anything other than a refusal to be rational. For the most part, reason is a trustworthy guide, and we ignore its counsel to our cost.

But reason will have its limits, for although it can be used in infinite ways — we can always find something new to think about — it can give us knowledge only of finite things — a thunderstorm, a chemical reaction, a legal principle. By definition, reason cannot know, except through vague, speculative analogy, what lies beyond its borders. A few centuries after Ghazali, the mystical poet Shabistari (c. 1250–1320) took up the theme of reason's blindness in his poem *The Secret Rose Garden*:

As the man blind from birth
Believes not nor understands

Your description of colours,
Even if you showed him proofs for a century,
So blind reason cannot see the future state.
But beyond reason man has a certain knowledge
Which God has placed in his soul and body
Whereby he perceives the hidden mysteries.[6]

To see the future state and to perceive the hidden mysteries is a privilege that belongs only to a special class of people – prophets, saints and great spiritual teachers – who transcend reason through a holy, prophetic spirit. Some of us will doubt that such a prophetic spirit exists because we have no experience of it. But that, Ghazali insisted, was as absurd as the tone-deaf man who declares that there is no such thing as music just because he himself cannot hear it. We may not deny the truth of mysticism just because we ourselves have not received it. If we have doubts, let us be generous enough to imagine a knowledge that exceeds reason. Such knowledge can lead to a direct experience of God, which explains why Ghazali called true mystics 'those who have arrived': they are completely absorbed within the supreme being and are at one with its unity. They have arrived at the summit of comprehension, and know all that there is to be known.

Disappointingly, few among us will fully transcend reason, at least here on earth. To illustrate the difference between the many (who are bound by reason's shackle) and the few (who break free of it), Ghazali uses the image of a nut. Just as a nut comprises an outer husk, an inner rind, a kernel and precious oil that can be extracted from the kernel, religious believers are similarly varied. The husk represents those who profess belief but lack conviction, and so their faith exists on the surface level; the inner rind stands for all those who have a sincere faith, but one which they have accepted on mere hearsay from parents and teachers; the kernel signifies those who have a more personal faith but are still attached to the world; the oil extracted from the kernel symbolises something truly rare: the mystic whose faith is pure, in the same way that almond oil is the pure essence of the almond.

Most of us, says Ghazali, will never get beyond the inner rind. In other words, while everyone is called to observe religious law, only a few will penetrate to the law's inner meaning and thus apprehend the mystic virtues. Only to these devout few is the mystic way open, and only they can re-orient their lives in pursuit of the more exalted virtues that contain the hidden meaning of the lower ones.

Beyond the mountains

Mystics in all traditions, not just Islam, describe their experience as following a path. Frequently, this path is vertical – an ascent – to emphasise that the mystic strives for improvement, moral refine-ment and the apprehension of higher truths. The path is a path to be climbed, for it begins with the lower self but ends in union with God, the highest reality. The upward journey is arduous and, like a mountain climber struggling to reach the next crevice or ledge on the rocky surface, we struggle to acquire virtue in the midst of life's harshness.

Many passages from the Koran hold a mystical significance for Sufis, and in such passages they find esoteric, hidden meanings about the nature of the path or ascent. It is not difficult to imagine studying the Koran for secret meanings since it was traditionally committed to memory (especially at a time when literacy was not widespread) and then recited, both silently and aloud. The Koran was ever present in the believer's mind – living inside one's head, so to speak – and thus a constant source of inspiration. Passages that might be passed over in reading could be dwelt upon at length through memory, fuelling the imagination and giving rise to ever deeper and more complex inter-pretations.

The Sufis were inspired by the story of Muhammad's mystical ascent to heaven, and regarded it as a founding example of the Sufi path and a model for religious seekers throughout the ages. One night, while in a meditative trance, the prophet was carried on the back of a winged horse called Buraq, first to the ruined Temple of Solomon in Jerusalem (where he prayed with the prophets Abraham, Moses and Jesus) and then upward to the Seventh Heaven. The site of the ascent is marked by the Dome of the Rock, the holiest shrine in Islam outside Mecca. Symbolically, the heavenward ascent stands for the journey of humanity to its outermost limit, where it stands on the threshold of transcendent reality and final meaning. It signifies that worldly attachments – and more than that, worldly experiences and ways of understanding – have been left far behind. To describe the ascent in words is already to betray it, to create a false rendering, because the experience itself surpasses the boundaries of human language. Words can only fail to convey the highest reality.

And yet we must make do with words, for that is all we have. We need not despair, however, since poetry has long been a way for words to hint at something beyond themselves, some dimension of truth which they cannot fully capture but only latch on to for a fleeting moment. So when the Sufis wanted to describe the mystical ascent, they used the language of symbols and images. In the West, the most widely known work of Sufi poetry is *The Rubaiyat* of Omar Khayyam. But the greatest allegorical expression of the Sufi path is found in an epic poem of 5,000 lines written in the twelfth century by another Persian writer, the sometime pharmacist Fariduddin Attar. This inspirational classic is called *The Conference of the Birds*. It is no accident that the story is about birds, for the bird is an ancient symbol of the human soul, which can be either caged or set free.

As the poem begins, the birds of the world realise that they are the only creatures who lack a supreme ruler, and so they decide to search for one. They elect a hoopoe bird to guide them in their quest. The hoopoe is no ordinary bird, for he had been entrusted by King Solomon to carry messages to the Queen of Sheba. On his head he bears a crest of feathers to signify his attainment of spiritual wisdom, and on his beak is written the word *Bismillah* ('in the name of God'), the first word of the Koran. The hoopoe symbolises our need for the guidance of a spiritual master (*shaykh*) as we make our inner journey to enlightenment and happiness.

Assuming his role as guide and mentor, the hoopoe warns the other birds that the journey ahead is arduous and long. More encouragingly, he also tells them that the journey will be worthwhile because the birds *do* have a king. His name is Simurgh, and he lives at the end of the world, beyond the mountains of Kaf. To reach their mysterious king, the birds must pass through seven valleys, each with its own dangers. At first, the birds rejoice; but some of them quickly succumb to despair and doubt. A few back out of the journey before it begins, protesting that it would be too difficult, or that finding their king doesn't really matter. The nightingale is the first to refuse, since he cannot bear to be parted from his beloved, the rose. The hawk decides to stay the servant of its royal master, while the duck is content to paddle away in the river.

The reluctant birds represent those of us who are so attached to worldly goods that we cannot even begin our spiritual journey, let alone awaken to a higher reality. Like the nightingale, we mistake the passing beauty of the world for God's eternal beauty; like the hawk, we mistake mankind's temporal authority for God's everlasting rule. And just as the duck proudly swears that he is clean because he spends all his time in water, we delude ourselves into believing that our souls are already pure, and so we need make no more effort. In the birds' unwillingness to embark on the journey we are meant to see the reflection of our own anxieties and fears about the path to inner wisdom. Part of us wants to set out on this path, for we all yearn to be united with something greater than ourselves. Yet another part shrinks back in fear, knowing that to complete the journey we must abandon all the things that seem most precious to us.

Not all the birds, however, are scared, and the resolute ones begin the journey. Some falter along the way, and to embolden them the hoopoe tells stories of what they can expect in each of the seven valleys. After many years, they pass through the valleys and finally reach Simurgh's palace. Only thirty birds remain. The seven valleys are the seven steps along the Sufi path, or the ascending stages of the soul as it progresses towards perfect happiness. They include the renunciation of worldly goods, detachment from desire and the recognition of the unity of all things. In more modern idiom, we could say that the valleys represent moments of greater and greater enlightenment of our consciousness.

Has the journey been worth the effort? And just who is Simurgh, the king that the thirty birds have sought? The answer lies within the name itself, for in Persian *simurgh* means 'thirty birds'. (For the Sufis, wordplay is not a trick, but a means of conveying a true yet secret meaning.) When the thirty birds finally enter the palace to meet their true king, they discover, to their astonishment, that they are Simurgh and Simurgh is themselves:

> There in the Simurgh's radiant face they saw
> Themselves, the Simurgh of the world – with awe
> They gazed, and dared at last to comprehend
> They were the Simurgh and the journey's end.[7]

The moment when the birds look at their king and see themselves staring back is a moment not of selfish arrogance but its opposite: the absorption of the self into the fullest reality. That is the moment, so longed for, of spiritual awakening, and the realisation of a deeper, more profound reality within this life. Like the thirty birds, we, too, can penetrate to the heart of things, to the essence of truth, and see cosmic unity everywhere, including within ourselves. Parallels to other religious traditions spring immediately to mind, whether the profound silence that overtook Aquinas in his final days or the Hindu teaching that ultimate reality is everywhere, like a grain of salt dissolved in water.

Attar's poem is enchanting and entertaining, but that is not its purpose. Its purpose is to illuminate, to show us a picture of life more penetratingly real than could be achieved through book learning and cold logic. The story of the birds should spark within us a flash of intuitive insight, the merest beginning of mystical perception. The poem's value lies not in the story that it tells but in the strength of our response to it. Like all Sufi poetry, it was meant to be recited, and the listener must listen out of longing for contact with something greater, not desire for pleasure or amusement. You listen to the poet's words, but what you hear – what enters you – is the voice of God.

Overcoming the self

As the birds near the end of their long journey, they ask the hoopoe what gift they should give to Simurgh. He tells them to present the king with something that cannot be found in his court. What could that be, the birds wonder, for surely so great a king lacks for nothing. Not so, says the hoopoe; there are two things unknown in Simurgh's realm: a heart filled with longing and a soul in torment.

The lesson for us is clear: we embark on the mystic path not because we are strong – and thus can endure it – but because we are weak – and thus need it. The inward journey arises out of our weakness, out of our desire to overcome the lack within us. Paradoxically, these negative, empty feelings are precisely what make us poised for happiness. For only by acknowledging this deficit of the soul can we ever move beyond it.

The desire to move beyond our own limitations leads on to the story's deeper lesson: that we are captive to a false sense of identity and must overcome it in order to arrive at our true self. The great Sufi poet Jalal al-Din Rumi (1207–73) wrote, in a way that at first seems puzzling, about the need to die to ourselves in order to become ourselves:

> I, being self-confined,
> Self did not merit,

Till, leaving self behind,
Did self inherit.[8]

As Rumi tells us, the egoistic manner in which we are conditioned, or accustomed, to understand ourselves ('being self-confined') is illusory – although to us it does not seem that way. Indeed, the illusion seems the most real thing that we know. But that is only because we have not yet gained the wisdom to see beyond it. We are like the dreamer who mistakes the dream for reality: the actual reality is there all the time, but we have not yet woken up to it.

At the risk, perhaps, of some confusion, we could say that the self is the self's problem. Or, to put it in modern psychoanalytic terms, the *ego* is the self's problem. We have seen this before, most vividly in the Buddhist belief that the ego is a trap, and that the defensive project of 'self-image' needs to be dismantled. In a similar way, Sufi mystics believe that the problem self – the unhappy self – is the one enslaved by desire and governed by base instincts and appetites. They teach that while we know (and have known all along) what is right, we keep inclining towards the wrong, like a ship that has lost its moorings.

Yet even in that bewildered state, the mystics assure us, we perceive, however dimly, that something is amiss; that somehow this accustomed 'self' is inauthentic and needs correction. Sensing the falseness within, we yearn for truth to take its place. We feel our own insincerity as a wound, the wound of absence. Yet this act of self-reproach – the heart filled with longing, the soul in torment, the unhappy self – is precisely what gets us on our way. From the wreck of reproach we salvage hope. Dismayed though we are by our current self, we know that we are but the prelude to an eventually transformed self. Who we *would* be, we *can* be.

It is difficult to express in a literal way what it means to overcome the self, to deflate the ego. Buddha likened it to a flame that has been extinguished. For Aquinas, it was the realisation that all his writings were no better than straw. The Sufi poet Attar expressed it as the birds' recognition that they themselves were 'the Simurgh of the world'. The mutual identity shared by Simurgh and the thirty birds – which makes them in some way indivisible – reveals one of Sufism's core principles: that the individual self can be united, or integrated, with a reality beyond itself.

In trying to express this ineffable truth, Sufi writers have used other images – a river that empties into the ocean or a spark that falls back into the flame. The poet Rumi wrote of the reed flute, cut from the reed bed, whose plaintive sound expresses its yearning to return home. In the song of the flute we hear the cry of our lost unhappy soul. These are powerful ancient metaphors of the soul's journey back towards the divine creator from whom it has been separated.

The alchemy of happiness

Perhaps the greatest lesson we can learn from the Sufis is that whether we realise it or not, we are all searching for what is absent in our lives, dimly aware that we have been separated from the origin of our being. Thus, being in God's presence, beholding his face, is – for the Sufis – the supreme pleasure and ultimate end of human life. That is also what Aquinas meant when he wrote that happiness was contemplating the beatific vision. While Christianity teaches that perfect happiness exists only in heaven, Islam teaches that a direct encounter with God's essence can occur during a lifetime – but that such a supreme experience is granted only to the prophets, the saints and the Sufi masters.

Though most of us are incapable of reaching the higher mystical states, the mere awareness of their existence can help us to refocus our lives in a more honest way; to begin working on the self-transformation that Ghazali called 'the alchemy of happiness'. The name Ghazali, in some variants, means 'the spinner', and it is tempting to read it as yet another symbol of self-transformation. Like the spinner who turns raw materials into something finished and fine, the spiritual teacher Ghazali takes coarse humanity and 'spins' it into a state of moral refinement.

Because the Sufi path awakens us to an *inner* reality, there is always the risk that the aspirant will misinterpret that reality because he is unprepared for it, or will succumb to emotional hysteria and self-delusion. As a safeguard, the aspirant entrusts himself to a spiritual teacher in a Sufi order to oversee the process of his transformation. Under the teacher's guidance, the novice stays true to the path and does not lead himself into selfishness or error. The Sufi orders, which arose in the twelfth century, are not monastic orders, such as found in Christianity, but fellowships, or confraternities, of those who have chosen to follow the Sufi path. Each order has developed a particular outward form of undertaking the inner journey, a particular set of actions that elicit an ecstatic response – a state of exaltation – which brings the Sufi closer to God's presence.

The most famous of the Sufi orders is the Mevlevi, whose members are known throughout the West as the 'Whirling Dervishes', because of the distinctive dance they perform as a means of concentration. (The dervishes spend 1,001 days learning the dance by spinning around a large nail placed between the first two toes of the left foot.) As they become absorbed within the spinning motion of the dance, the dervishes feel the boundaries of the self begin to melt away. The dancers wear black cloaks that they cast off, revealing white garments underneath. The symbolism is far from obscure: the dance is a mystical journey from the death of the self to resurrection in union with God. It is something more than a cliché to state that the dervishes lose themselves in the dance.

For Westerners, particularly, it is easy to be distracted by the exoticism of the Sufi orders, especially when they are as thrilling as the Whirling Dervishes. But nothing would be a greater betrayal of Sufism than to focus exclusively on the outward form of its practices – the dancing, the spinning, the howling – for that is to neglect the inner meaning. Silence, just as much as frenzy, can be a sign of mystic insight, a way of experiencing transcendent happiness here on earth (as Aquinas, in his final days, must have known). Such has been the teaching of the great Sufi masters for the past thousand years. Always, our goal must be what lies underneath the world of appearance, what is largely hidden from view.

The stages of the Sufi path vary according to the teacher (who recognises that each of us must walk his own path), but they always begin with repentance and culminate in an emptying of the self so that it can be absorbed in a reunion with God. What all the paths and mystic teachings have in common is the quest for unity, and the soul's desire to find happiness by merging with something beyond itself. We can feel this call for unity most powerfully in the emotional extravagance of Sufi poetry. Drunkenness is the most unlikely, and yet the most suggestive, image of spiritual ecstasy and the joy of being united with God. But more important than euphoria is the altered state of consciousness, the slipping away of the self, when we are absorbed into the divine unity. Just as the drunkard loses self-control – his speech is slurred, his movements shaky and unbalanced – the mystic gradually surrenders his ego, allowing the self to be annihilated.

The great Sufi poets are not teaching that intoxication is the path to wisdom and happiness; rather, they are speaking figuratively, using words to express a truth that words cannot actually convey. All mystic poetry relies upon this sort of negative aesthetic, for it reaches out to something beyond itself, something which language can only hint at. Paradoxically, then, the true meaning of Sufi poetry lies in what the words *fail* to say. As the medieval poet Shabistari put it:

> For within the mere words and sounds
> Of the mystic song
> Lies a precious mystery.[9]

For some of us, however, the precious mystery will remain a mystery. We hear the poet's words, but are deaf to their meaning. How can we talk about mysticism in a world that is not prepared for it? Spiritual states are visible in ways that are easily misunderstood:

ecstatic utterances, wild movements or fixed trances. When the 'drunken' mystic Bayazid (d. 875) exclaimed 'Glory be to me!', he was accused of blasphemy because the literal meaning of his words was offensive to his fellow Muslims: he made a god of himself. Such utterances cannot be understood literally but only metaphorically. To those who cannot appreciate them in this way, mystic insights will seem, at best, mere nonsense and, at worst, the dangerous doings of a heretic.

And yet mystic visions are as real as the things we experience in the world, but real in a different way. The reality they disclose cannot be demonstrated through scientific experiment, but only perceived by the imagination. Thus, for the mystic, a vision that he creates is an earthly manifestation of a truth that exists more perfectly in the divine sphere. Neither indulging a fantasy nor telling a lie, the mystic conjures up in this world something that originates in an immaterial, transcendent realm.

If interpreted literally, Sufi poetry and ecstatic practices will confuse, perhaps threaten, anyone who does not possess the knowledge or disposition necessary to understand their symbolic force. Not everyone is prepared to find ultimate truth – or happiness, or enlight-enment – through their own imagination. Many of us simply want to be told – first by parents and teachers, and later by superiors and insti-tutional authorities – what is true, what is right and what to believe. What we don't want is to doubt, to ask questions. So to anyone who blindly accepts a secondhand faith – mere hearsay – the mystic path will seem strewn with error.

As Junayd understood, it is dangerous to speak of such things too loudly, too openly, because other people – the uninitiated – are bound to misunderstand them, and that could lead to suspicion and alarm. Because spiritual states are essentially private, it is impossible for anyone on the outside to enter into that experience. Nobody but you can really know what is happening inside you. And so even to write about the mystic search for happiness, particularly in a general sense (as I have been doing), is already to depart from it, already to slant it in a misleading way. Sufism is really not something that anyone can learn about; it is something that must be experienced from the inside.

'A walnut for everyone who slaps me'

Upon first acquaintance, mysticism has a surprisingly modern feel. It values personal experience, expresses the freedom of the individual and looks suspiciously upon all things regimented and doctrinaire. It sits harmoniously with our reigning desire to be liberated. This may well explain why, nearly a thousand years after Ghazali wrote it, *The Alchemy of Happiness* still strikes a chord with readers, including – especially – those in the secular West. Yet in other respects, the mystic path to happiness is not easy to understand, let alone follow. It does not conform to our rational, empirical mindset; it presumes that everyone believes in a God; it takes long periods of training and apprenticeship. In a quick-fix culture, the patient nurturing of insight into a higher reality will scarcely seem worth the effort. We want happiness, but we want it now.

Despite suspiciously easy parallels with 'New Age' seekers, mysticism (of whatever origin) must strike us as the invention of an alien culture: one that regards people as inherently unequal, at least in terms of their ability to apprehend the fundamental truth of things. The distinction between the ignorant many and the knowledgeable few is the aspect of mysticism most at odds with Western democratic values and an ingrained belief in equality. There is no getting around the fact, uncomfortable though it may be, that the mystic view of happiness is elitist. It is not that the mystics are deliberately seeking to prevent most of us from becoming happy, but that true happiness can come only to those select few who are versed in the ways of imagination and intuition. Only they will know the highest form of bliss because only they will know the inner meaning of outward appearance.

It did not bother Ghazali that some people were forever barred from perfect happiness. Otherwise he would not have told the following story. Bayazid, the famous 'drunken' Sufi, was approached by an unhappy man who protested that he had fasted and prayed for thirty years yet was no closer to finding spiritual joy. The mystic told him that not even three hundred years would be time enough. 'Why?' the man asked. 'Because your selfishness stands between you and God.' Desperate, the man pleaded to be taught how to surmount the obstacle of his own selfishness. Bayazid told him that there was indeed a way forward, but it would be impossible to follow. The man insisted that he be told. Relenting, Bayazid commanded him to shave his beard, wear only a loincloth, put on a feeding bag full of walnuts, and then stand in the marketplace, shouting, 'A walnut for everyone who slaps me'. If he could do that, then he might find some happiness. The man scoffed at the suggestion, just as Bayazid knew he would. And yet as the Sufi master added, there was no other way.

We are the man who refuses to stand in the marketplace and be slapped. Like him, we cannot imagine how to become happy. And imagination is the secret. When the path to happiness is laid out for us we reject it as ridiculous and humiliating. It seems to be not within our power to move from ignorance to knowledge, from misery to happiness.

But perhaps that is too darkly pessimistic a view. We cannot all be mystics, nor would we want to be; but we can try to preserve and honour something of their spirit in our lives. We can begin to see through the world of appearances into a deeper reality. The deeds and testament of Ghazali, the sublime verse of medieval Islamic poets and the arresting practices of Sufi disciples still hold the power to inspire. Such things are not cold to the touch. We cannot know of them and remain unmoved. Even if all we take away from them is a glimmering of some greater happiness, still that may be enough – for a glimmering is a hopeful promise of what is yet to come.

Part IV
Enduring Suffering

7

It's All in Your Mind
(The Stoics)

A man with a broken leg is a natural Stoic. In 1992, Admiral James B. Stockdale came to national attention in the United States when he was named Ross Perot's running-mate on an independent ticket in that year's presidential election. (At the polls, Bill Clinton ousted the incumbent, George H.W. Bush.) An unwilling aspirant to national office, Stockdale (who died in July 2005) was, by temperament and appearance, ill-suited for the slick media exchanges that pass for political discourse today. On screens throughout America he came across as precisely the man he was: a cantankerous, white-haired sea dog who walked with a pronounced limp.

The limp resulted from an old war injury. During the Vietnam War, Stockdale was a carrier-based fighter pilot with the US Navy, in command of Air Wing 16. Since the start of the war he had flown nearly 200 successful combat missions south of Hanoi. But on the 9th of September 1965, his luck ran out. Pulling out of his dive after bombing a cargo train, he was shot down by enemy fire. He parachuted out of his plane, and broke his leg as he fell to the ground.

Upon landing, he was captured by the North Vietnamese. Along with the ten other members of his crew, he remained their prisoner for eight years. As Stockdale explains in his memoirs, his captors used physical torture – isolation, handcuffs and leg-irons – to break his will. The torments would stop, he was told, if he went on television to condemn the war and denounce America's political establishment. Although he suffered greatly, Stockdale refused to break. During the first few years of his imprisonment he could not stand upright because of his injured leg. He was forced into solitary confinement for four years, during which time he communicated with the other American prisoners in adjoining cells by tapping out code on the wall.

Stockdale attributed his survival, both physical and mental, to the teachings of the Stoic philosopher Epictetus (c. AD 50–130). When Stockdale had been a graduate student at Stanford, his philosophy professor gave him a copy of Epictetus' *Enchiridion*, a short manual on how to lead the Stoic life. At first, the young military officer doubted the value of this collection of ancient philosophical precepts. (Was he not taught that Frederick the Great always went into battle with a copy at his side?) Yet as he lay suffering with a fractured leg, Stockdale drew strength from Epictetus' assertion that 'lameness is an impediment to the body but not to the will'. This was no abstract principle of the moral imagination issued by someone sheltered from real-life hardship. On the contrary. Epictetus knew what he wrote about: when he was still a servant, his master, in an act of sheer cruelty, broke both his legs, crippling him for life.

The example of Epictetus helped Stockdale to realise the Stoic truth that happiness is the virtue of indifference to whatever is beyond our control. For him, Stoic detachment was uncannily applicable to his own misfortune: his North Vietnamese captors could imprison his body but never his mind. And as long as he preserved freedom in his mind, then he really was free. Physical captivity, however agonising, could not deprive him of his liberty. The constant and heroic Admiral Stockdale is a humbling modern example of philosophy's ancient power to help us endure unimaginable misery and suffering. Yet it is equally, and encouragingly, true that Stoicism can appeal to those of us who suffer in more ordinary ways, who feel the day-to-day struggle just to survive can be affliction enough.

Born in adversity

As befits a school of thought that helps its adherents to prepare for the worst, Stoicism was born in that most harrowing of circumstances, a shipwreck. Headed elsewhere, the maritime passenger Zeno of Cittium (334–262 BC) was forced to land in Athens, a place which evidently earned his loyalty, for he lived there until his death fifty years later. The young man already possessed a spirit of detachment, for upon learning that his possessions were lost at sea, he calmly replied, 'Fortune bids me be less encumbered.' Once settled into Athenian life, the unencumbered Zeno began to study philosophy, the city's most celebrated commodity.

No admirer of Epicurus (who had returned to Athens a few years earlier), he believed that happiness should be based on reason, not pleasure. Rejecting the hedonist's obsession with individual desire, Zeno insisted that the wise man was not free to ignore his duties and obligations towards others. Living the good life meant throwing yourself into society, however troubling and messy that turned out to be. It was a sign of Zeno's commitment to the general welfare that he taught not in seclusion (as Epicurus did) but in the Stoa Poecile, a public structure that consisted of a long painted colonnade with an adjoining courtyard. Stoicism took its name from this place where Zeno – who preferred colonnades because he had a habit of pacing up and down while teaching – instructed his first pupils.

The Stoic's concern for others made the good life a rather unpredictable affair, since it entailed dealing with the changing, often disordered, circumstances of other people's lives. Among Zeno's followers, Panaetius of Rhodes (185–110 BC) understood especially well that moral standards could not exist apart from the actual circumstances of everyday life. As Stoicism migrated from democratic Athens to republican (and then imperial) Rome, it increasingly adopted this more pragmatic outlook. Stoicism spares no time for dwelling upon moods or wallowing in feelings because there is urgent business to be done. The Stoic must learn how to cope not just with life's ordinary ups and downs but with its major traumas – death and bereavement, the loss of status or reputation and worries about money and health. As well, he must learn to cope with success, for good fortune carries its burdens, as any paparazzi-hounded celebrity will self-pitifully cry.

Although criticised for being more a coping mechanism than a fully articulated philosophy, Stoicism has been the West's most enduring philosophy of consolation. Repudiating, as it does, the power of a brutal world to make anyone unhappy, Stoicism has always appealed to those who live in dark times. Its lasting influence has been secured not by the totality of its principles (no such totality exists) but by the recurrence of misfortune that makes Stoic principles perennially relevant. There has never been a shortage of people who suffer; there has only been a shortage of ways to comfort them. Stoicism meets the shortfall by bending and shaping itself to the different crises that arise in different historical moments, from the murderous political intrigues of the classical world to the terrorist attacks of the new millennium.

Driven, always, by contemporary events, Stoicism naturally captures the tenor of the times. In ancient Rome it provided the guiding ethical framework for morally upright public officials – here, we must remember Seneca – who were obliged to serve tyrants and despots. To those frightened by the religious wars that overtook Europe in the sixteenth century, Stoicism appeared as a welcome source of moral instruction and refuge from civil strife. When our lives today become turbulent and unpredictable we might profitably turn to Stoicism because it will help us to withstand all that is turbulent and unpredictable. When we feel that too much of what we face day after day is beyond our control, we might well take heart in the Stoic teaching that happiness resides only in those things we *can* control: our thoughts, intentions and outlooks. Stoicism does not stop bad things from happening (no philosophy could) but it helps us to cope when they do happen and to remember that we can still be happy when misfortune clouds our life.

All you need is virtue

Cicero summed up Stoic ethics in the (for him) paradoxical belief that 'virtue is all you need for happiness'. If, in any situation, you are inclined to do the morally right thing (which is what virtue means), then you will be happy – always and automatically, no matter what befalls you, or what does not. Amidst all the vicissitudes of life, only virtue will bring you lasting contentment.

As Cicero knew only too well, this proposition clashed with Aristotle's more commonsensical, more forgiving, view that external goods (health, wealth, etc.) are required for happiness because they enable us to put our virtue into action. Without them, Aristotle said, virtue can't really get started. To insist, then, that virtue – which is an inward disposition – is sufficient for happiness is to insist that nothing in the external world can affect our happiness, neither augmenting nor diminishing it. The outside world leaves no mark on our happiness; such is the Stoic view.

But suppose that happiness *were* vulnerable to forces in the external world. The consequences would be depressing. If our happiness depended upon favourable circumstances – random good luck – then we could never be sure of finding it, no matter how virtuous we were. Uncertain of the future, we could only, as Cicero put it, 'pray heaven that happiness might somehow come our way'.[1] And as we wait for Dame Fortune to locate us on her Global Positioning System, we will eventually conclude that there is no virtue to being virtuous. True, we might one day stumble upon happiness – it could be no more calculated than that – but it would not be virtue that made us stumble.

If happiness really does entail the possession of goods that depend partly on chance – health, wealth, fame and success – then it would be a rarity in human history since most people who have ever lived on this planet have not enjoyed the opportunities for upward mobility that we take as our birthright. Can this really be the sort of happiness that anyone wants? Why should happiness be a locked door that might (or might not) spring open and let us slip through to the other side? The happiness we wish for is a happiness that, however difficult to achieve, does not disqualify anyone from trying. For the Stoics (and most likely for us, too), happiness must be open to everyone on equal terms, accessible to all in the circumstances of life as it is lived here and now. Only then, because we have made the effort to obtain it, can we say that our happiness is not in jeopardy but safe and secure. It is something we 'own' and not just something we chance upon, like a shiny penny in the street.

To use a favoured Stoic analogy, we can no more command events in the world than the sailor can alter the direction of the wind. But our happiness does not thereby suffer, because it does not depend upon events in the world; it depends only upon the 'brilliance' of our virtue, as Cicero put it, a brilliance that no turn of worldly events could obscure or overwhelm.[2] No misfortune, no run of bad luck, will ever destroy or overthrow our happiness. No matter how much misery a happy man endures, he remains happy. (Epicurus believed the same, but for reasons that were more about the durability of pleasure.) The Stoic secret of happiness is that it lies in possessing only those things that fortune cannot steal from us, and those things always come down to good character.

Now that is an astounding proposition, and one that we are likely to greet with scepticism, if not downright dismissal. Even the ancients felt unsure about it, for they debated the question endlessly. Let us imagine, as they did, a happy person – that is, virtuous person – who is unjustly imprisoned and savagely beaten by his captors. A Stoic will argue that this person remains happy throughout his imprisonment, even at the very moment when the punches and blows fall upon him. Certainly, he feels the agony of his torments and wishes them to stop, for he is only human; but no torment, however severe, can rob him of his happiness. As Cicero confidently declared, happiness 'will not tremble, however much it is tortured'.[3] That was exactly the attitude that Stockdale took towards his suffering in the prison camps of North Vietnam. Less invitingly, the Stoic principle works the other way around – no amount of good fortune will make you happy. When an unhappy man wins the lottery, he stays unhappy: rich, but miserable.

Many of us, however, probably believe that things other than virtue are good, and thus likely to be sources of happiness: health, wealth, pleasure, honour, talent, beauty and brains. If such properties really are good, then happiness can arise from any of them (or disappear if any is taken away) and need not depend solely upon virtue. To counter that view, a Stoic would argue that such things are *not* good, at least not intrinsically so, because they can be used for either good or bad purposes; they can either help or harm. In fact, nearly everything we might assume to be morally good turns out to be morally *neutral*. Example: a rich man can use his wealth to be a philanthropist or to support terrorism. Each enterprise requires money, but the money itself is morally neutral. What matters is the individual's intention, be it moral or immoral.

By the same token, supposedly 'bad' things turn out to be morally neutral. Just as health and wealth are not inherently good, poverty and disease are not inherently bad. No reasonable person, a modern-day Stoic would claim, concludes that someone is immoral just because he cannot afford to pay his electricity bill. He might be ill, or unemployed, or barely able to feed and clothe his children. Our delinquent bill-payer could still be immoral, but it would have to be for reasons other than his failure to add to the profits of the utilities industry. Similarly, only a bigot – a person swayed by irrational fears – would denounce someone as immoral just for being HIV positive. If such a person were immoral, it would, again, have to be for different reasons. Although hard-line politicians on both the left and the right do their best to convince us otherwise, to be poor or sick is no moral failure. Yet as the wise Reb Tevye sardonically remarked in *Fiddler on the Roof*, it's no great honour, either.

Still, no rational person chooses to be destitute rather than solvent, ill rather than well. (It is precisely through such choices that we demonstrate our rationality.) Experience alone tells us that we do not, in fact, regard all morally neutral things as equally desirable: generally, we seek to enjoy health and wealth and to avoid sickness and poverty.

The Stoics made precisely that distinction. They rounded up all the supposedly good (but actually morally neutral) things in life and placed them in the special category of 'preferred indifferents'. Everything put in this category enhances our quality of life – and thus is preferred – but is not good in itself – and thus is morally indifferent. We like having preferred indifferents, and we are right to like them, because they smooth out life's rough edges. Many people in major cities have lived through the nightmare of getting to the airport on public transportation: fighting crowds of commuters while struggling to carry large heavy suitcases. How immeasurably more pleasant to take a taxicab (and to be able to afford it). The taxicab is one of modern life's great preferred indifferents, along with penicillin and personal trainers. Such things, although they do not make us virtuous, make us feel better; and if we are feeling better, we might find it a little bit easier to behave better. As today's Stoic knows, you are much less likely to lose your temper in a roomy, air-conditioned taxicab than in a crowded, stinking and stiflingly hot commuter train.

The wise man, as Seneca understood, knows how to handle preferred indifferents: he neither seeks 'Fortune's bounty' nor rejects it, nor mourns its loss.[4] (In writing that, Seneca was answering his critics, who had charged that he enjoyed unmerited wealth and power simply because he was in Emperor Nero's good graces.) Similarly, the wise man tolerates illness and injury, yet all the while wishes that he were healthy – not for the sake of health alone, but for the sake of all the good and useful things a healthy person can accomplish. This is the chief merit of all preferred indifferents, and the reason it is honourable to prefer them: they afford us more opportunity to act virtuously. So it is right and natural and wise (although not, strictly speaking, necessary) to seek wealth and health and strength. Indeed, the Stoics believed that it was better for a wise man than a fool to be wealthy, since the wise man would use his wealth to perform good deeds while the fool would not know how.

Smile at the raging storm

Neither desiring – nor despising – morally neutral things, the Stoic takes in his stride whatever comes his way, be it pleasure or pain, reward or punishment. It is wisdom to remain steadfast and even-tempered in the face of changing, uncontrollable events. (It wasn't just Seneca who learned that lesson but also Prince Arjuna.) So when fortune smiles upon us we must not delude ourselves into believing that its blessings will last for ever; when misfortunes arise, as inevitably they will, we can take heart in knowing that they, too, will run their course. The Stoic does not fear misfortune because misfortune is not evil. Come what may, we preserve our equanimity and look upon good and bad times alike with the same firm, dispassionate resolve, the same fearless, bold indifference.

As Admiral Stockdale knew firsthand, the power to persevere comes from within the mind. Like a fortress unassailable, it can grant us everlasting refuge (so the Stoics claim) from pain and adversity – and from the equally hazardous temptations of fame and glory. The citadel of the mind is breached only by the power of reason, as Hamlet, in meditative mood, understood only too well: 'Nothing is good or ill but thinking makes it so.' We cannot steer events in the outside world, or even always anticipate them; what we can do is to accept them, whatever they turn out to be, with calm, intelligent reason. Only then might we attain freedom in a world dominated by events unbiddable and unpredictable.

There is more than a touch of Stoicism in the Hindu and Buddhist principle of detachment from the fruits of our labours. In harmony with Eastern spiritual traditions, Stoicism does not ask us to renounce the world, but to be independent of it; to be immune to its charms and seductions no less than to its taunts and threats. We gain that independence, that freedom, by protecting ourselves from circumstances that we are powerless to control. And that is why the ancient Stoics devised exercises of restraint and self-control to steel themselves against injury and loss.

Many of these exercises will seem to us strange and harsh. When angry, hold a mirror in front of your face and look in disgust upon your distorted features. You will never want to be angry again. (Seneca liked that one.) A Stoic technique that hints at modern cognitive therapy is to 'relabel' unpleasant experiences. If trapped in a crowd, just think of it as a party – and then your emotions will change along with your thoughts. Other exercises have a touch of the morbid. Epictetus instructed his pupils to dwell on the thought, as they kissed their wives and children, that their loved ones were mortal and one day would die. When that day came they would be ready for it.

But do not suppose that the Stoic's detachment renders him heartless, for his emotions run as deeply as anyone's, his pleasures feel as intense, his pains equally acute. Shakespeare, again, shows us the emotional complexity of the Stoic hero. When Macduff, the stalwart soldier, learns the devastating news that Macbeth's henchman has slaughtered his entire family, his comrade urges him to bear his grief like a man. He retorts, wisely and humanely, that he must also 'feel it like a man'. Macduff honours (but does not indulge) his feelings by using them as a spur to virtuous action, for no sooner does grief come upon him than he moves to plot the downfall of the tyrannous Macbeth.

In the same way, the Stoic sage uses reason to keep his feelings in check, thus preventing any single-minded pursuit of pleasure or avoidance of pain. Indeed, as Seneca cautioned, some pleasures – 'blind and heedless devotion to one's affairs', 'wild elation deriving from trivial and childish causes', 'the idleness and decadence of a sluggish mind' – were simply corrupt.[5] Here, the contrast with Epicurus, for whom pleasure was the *dernier mot* of happiness, could not be stronger. Impassive in the face of pleasure and pain alike, the Stoic relies upon reason's trustworthy guidance.

Stoicism provides a firm basis not for solitude and renunciation (let Epicurus stay in his garden) but for direct action in the world. Recognising a duty to participate in civil society, the Stoic makes decisions without exclusive regard to self-interest. Detached, then, from his own immediate welfare, just as he is detached from his feelings, he fixes his attention on the wider social sphere. He is like a marksman aiming to hit a distant target.

That the Stoic cares for his neighbour is no accident. Through our rational powers, we all possess, as Cicero observed, a divine spark. This commonality binds us each to the other, requiring that we treat everyone else as decently as we would treat ourselves. In this way, a necessary part of anyone's happiness is a concern for others. And so the concept of private ethics is alien to Stoic thought. No fundamental difference exists between the 'contemplative' life and the 'active' life because contemplation is how we prepare for action; it is the thinking that precedes the doing. Thus, when Seneca says that virtue will be found 'in the temples, the forum, the senate-house, standing in defence of the city walls, dusty and sunburnt, with calloused hands', he is linking it explicitly with public life.[6]

Precisely because it values the active life, Stoicism has appealed throughout history to statesmen, public servants and politicians. And since a core Stoic principle is that misfortune cannot diminish happiness, we can hardly be surprised that it has been the philosophy of choice for good people in an age of despots. In ancient Rome, Stoicism found a highly receptive audience in state officials obliged to do a tyrant's bidding. Tyranny, like all external forces, was to be looked upon with detachment and indifference. It was – and is – the way of the world that some leaders will be virtuous, some villainous. Yet throughout it all, the public servant soldiers on. Not for nothing was the Roman Stoic watch-cry *vivere militare* – 'to live is to be a soldier'. Facing with equal composure both freedom and despotism, and sustained by the knowledge that no imperial edict, no dictatorial fiat, could overthrow his happiness, the Stoic stands unshaken by liberty's fall and tyranny's rise.

Intimate with suffering

They knew how to suffer, the Roman Stoics. Especially those unfortunate enough to live close to the centre of power. Stoicism provided Cicero and Seneca with the intellectual basis for their opposition to autocratic rule, while for Marcus Aurelius it illuminated the virtuous path to be followed by a philosopher-king. With a characteristic Roman pragmatism (this culture's lasting achievement was the aqueduct), all three wanted to know how Stoicism could be practised. Did it lead to the good life? Could it comfort honest men forced to serve dishonest masters? The answers lie in the story of their lives.

The champion of liberty

When Cicero (106–43 BC), the great Roman statesman, thought about happiness he did so in frank awareness of the suffering he was called to endure in both his political and personal life. In 63 BC he was named consul, the highest public office in the Roman republic, the form of government to which, against all odds, he remained lastingly loyal. During his consulship Cicero learned that Cataline was plotting to overthrow the republic and set up a dictatorship. Such treachery could not be countenanced, and so he quickly arrested the conspirators and summarily sentenced them to death. Cicero temporarily saved the republic (although not even he could reverse the gradual slide into civil war), but at great personal cost: Julius Caesar, who sought to hasten the republic's downfall, was now his enemy. Caesar, in shrewd retaliation, accused Cicero of malfeasance when he ordered Cataline to be executed without a trial. Cicero was convicted of the charge and briefly exiled as his punishment. Upon returning to Rome he resumed his political career, but never again would he hold high public office.

Matters worsened during the civil war (49–44 BC), when Cicero supported Pompey, whom Caesar eventually defeated. Having backed the losing candidate, so to speak, Cicero faced the stark truth that he had no political future whatsoever and no alternative but to retire to his countryside villa in Tusculum. Scarcely a year later, Caesar – now established as dictator – granted him a full pardon. Make no mistake; this was no invitation to return to public office, but simply a confirmation that the humbled and exiled Cicero no longer posed a threat. A tyrant runs no risk in pardoning the powerless.

Or maybe just a little. After Brutus assassinated Caesar, Cicero argued for the restoration of his beloved republic. That was very much the wrong case to plead, and Cicero paid for his liberal opinion with his life. The triumvirate that wielded temporary power immediately after Caesar's death – Mark Antony, Octavius (the future Caesar Augustus) and Lepidus – decreed that Cicero must be killed. And so he was. With him died the dream of the Roman republic.

In Cicero's many moments of despair, what he desperately needed was a principle to live by. He found it in Stoicism, which he modified to create a distinctively personal philosophy. Welcoming the solace provided by the Stoic values of indifference, detachment and tranquillity, Cicero drew strength in dark times from his belief that philosophy 'takes away the load of empty troubles, sets us free from desires, [and] banishes fears'.[7]

But philosophy was no retreat from life; it was politics by other means. Through reading, thinking and writing Cicero could continue his public career even though barred from public office. In his essays, letters and dialogues he could express the same ideas, the same principles and the same tough practical wisdom that had guided his decisions when he had been an esteemed public servant. By so devoting himself to scholarship he embraced the Stoic belief that the contemplative life benefits society because it teaches us through reflection how best to act in the world. Like the fabled Stoic sage, Cicero rejected as irrational the view that thought and action were irreconcilable opposites:

> ... after serious and long continued reflection as to how I might do good to as many people as possible, and thereby prevent any interruption of my service to the State, no better plan occurred to me than to conduct my fellow-citizens in the ways of the noblest learning.[8]

This is philosophy – 'the ways of the noblest learning' – expounded by someone with a passion for the activity and energy of life, a passion felt all the more keenly when suddenly checked by rude fate. Forced, repeatedly, into exile or house arrest, Cicero was naturally drawn to a philosophy that prized equanimity: the ability to treat all things in the same manner, even-handed and controlled. Sharing the Stoic conviction that happiness was independent of chance events and circumstances, Cicero believed that 'a man who is capable of regarding all the hazards and accidents of fortune and human life as endurable' will have 'every reason' to find happiness.[9] He wrote about himself, preferring not to disguise his torments, and declared that his own banishment was no hardship. For the Stoic, all suffering is bearable.

The tyrant's tutor

Now is the time to take a longer look at Seneca's remarkable search for happiness in the midst of misfortune. He was banished to Corsica in AD 41 after the emperor Claudius' wife, that shameless hussy Messalina, falsely accused him of committing adultery with the emperor's niece, Julia Livilla. Seneca lived in miserable exile on the barren island for eight years. For the Romans, the pain of exile was worse than we can imagine, since it meant a complete loss of identity; in exile, a civilised man found himself cast out into the wilderness, forced to keep company with barbarians. Seneca's fortunes improved only when Claudius' next wife, the cunning Agrippina, sister to the defamed Julia Livilla, recalled him to Rome and appointed him tutor to her twelve-year-old son (from an earlier marriage) Lucius Domitius, the future emperor Nero. That moment sealed Seneca's fate, and swept him up in the turbulent affairs of an affable and popular young prince who went unbelievably bad.

In AD 54, so the gossipy historian Suetonius tells us, Agrippina, impatient for her son to ascend the imperial throne, killed Claudius by feeding him poisoned mushrooms. During the young Nero's tyrannical rule, Seneca became a leading statesman, enjoying unforeseen wealth, power and fame. Yet this prominence, which contrasted so sharply with the shame and disgrace of his years in exile, was a poisoned chalice, for it came at the price of having to submit to the emperor's every wish. Seneca was still Nero's slave; he was just a slave with unsurpassed influence. A mere five years into his reign, Nero, who had pledged himself so often to the virtue of clemency, renounced any pretence of goodness when he forced Seneca to plot the assassination of Agrippina – the emperor's own mother. Perhaps when Seneca received this damnable order he recalled Cicero's words of warning that nobody who values his freedom can serve a tyrant.

Imagine the turmoil Seneca must have felt when commanded to be an accessory to murder. After all, the dowager empress Agrippina was his patron: the woman who had secured his return from exile, had given him back his life. But neither was she the flower of maternal virtue; she had killed her husband and was rumoured to harbour incestuous desires for her son. Still, was this how Seneca would repay Agrippina's generosity, by conspiring to kill her? A further abomination awaited. Seneca was compelled to justify the murder before his fellow senators. In publicly excusing his crimes, Seneca dishonoured the state he had given his life to serve. But he showed no reluctance, no inclination to curb the emperor's violent instincts. Appalled by the brutality of imperial politics, and shamed by his complicity in them, Seneca retired three years later and vowed, bitterly, never to return to public life.

Yet even in retirement Seneca could not escape Nero's cruelty, and days that should have been peaceful were just as precarious and intrigue-filled as they had ever been. In AD 65, only a few years after withdrawing from politics Seneca was ordered to kill himself – an order that he carried out – because Nero suspected him of participating in a rebellious plot led by Calpurnius Piso. The evidence was flimsy (a letter to Piso expressing friendly sentiments), but it was enough to send Seneca to his death since Nero was hardly willing to let a possible adversary live, especially one who could expose all his dirty tricks.

Tacitus, never one to shy away from a shocker, dramatised Seneca's slow and painful death in his *Annals of Imperial Rome*. Because he regarded the suicide as an act of heroic defiance, the ancient historian modelled his account on the similarly courageous death of Socrates, as recorded in Plato's *Phaedo*. Like the Greek philosopher before him, Seneca faced death with neither fear nor sadness. To his friends, in whose cherished company he died, he bequeathed his only remaining possession: 'the pattern of my life'.[10] As the centurion bearing the death sentence stood by, their tears elicited from the doomed man not sympathy but a rebuke: What had become of the philosophy that should give them the strength to withstand misfortune? Had it now deserted them, when they most needed it? No one should be surprised by Nero's heartlessness, he calmly explained, for a man who murders his own mother will not think twice before killing someone as insignificant as his teacher. It would be no more to him than swatting a fly.

In his last moments, Seneca begged his wife, Paulina, to set a fixed term to her grief and console herself with the memory of his good deeds. Unwilling to live without her husband, Paulina insisted upon dying with him. Seneca praised her decision as nobler than his own because she had chosen to sacrifice her life, while he had no choice at all. Prepared to end their lives together, they cut open veins in their arms with a single stroke. Seneca, because of his infirmity, bled too slowly, and so he also severed the veins in his ankles and behind his knees. Wishing to spare his wife the gruesome sight of his mutilated body, he requested that she be removed to an adjoining chamber. Nero, fearful of making himself even more unpopular, ordered that Paulina's wounds be stanched and that she be kept alive; he would not grant her a martyr's glory.

The unsuspecting Seneca, now surrounded by his companions, drank a cup of poison. When that did not kill him, he immersed himself in a warm bath to accelerate the blood loss. (Rubens's painting of this moment is appropriately dignified, but gets every historical detail wrong, including the style of Seneca's beard and the size of his bathtub.) At last nearing death, he was carried into a steam room, where the vapours finally suffocated him. In accordance with the instructions he had dictated when at the height of his power, Seneca was cremated without pomp or ceremony.

Throughout his traumatically unbalanced life, Seneca endured fortune and misfortune, prominence and exile, reward and punish-ment; he was forced to kill others and, finally, to kill himself. If anyone had good cause to meditate upon the vagaries of life, it was he. He put his thoughts into writing, producing ten treatises on ethics that have survived solely because in the eleventh century the monks of Monte Cassino (the very place where the young Aquinas studied) transcribed them from a lost Latin manuscript. These works include: *De vita beata* ('On the Happy Life'); *De tranquillitate animi* ('On Peace of Mind'), whose very name affirms a Stoic virtue; the *Consolatio ad Helviam* ('The Consolation of Helvia'), a formal letter written to his widowed mother, Helvia, to lessen her grief during his Corsican exile; and *De clementia* ('On Mercy'). Was it crafty politics – or desperate hope – that led Seneca to dedicate 'On Mercy' to the eighteen-year-old Nero, then still young enough to learn a lesson in morality?

Over the centuries, Seneca has attracted countless readers because he has revealed that the secret of happiness (or at least *a* secret) is the power of the rational mind to triumph over adversity. But there is more: the secret turns out to be common knowledge. For it was 'nature's intention', he confidently explained, 'that there should be no need of great equipment for a good life: every individual can make himself happy'.[11] But Seneca also knew that some of his contemporaries (the Epicureans, most likely) dismissed Stoicism as a trick, or confidence game, which deceived us about the harsh realities of poverty, illness and suffering. It was simply disingenuous, his critics claimed, to teach (as Seneca did) that suffering was not actually suffering if we refused to accept it as such.

But I think that so negative a view misses Stoicism's central point, which is not to mask or trivialise suffering – but to give us the means of *enduring* it. Yes, Stoicism speaks to our feelings of misery, discontent and loneliness; but it speaks to them so that we need not be enslaved to them. If being happy meant anything to Seneca, it meant possessing 'a mind which is free, upright, fearless and unshakeable, untouched by fear or desire'.[12]

The philosopher-king

Seneca's problem was timing. He had the bad luck to live in an age of tyrants. Born a century later, he would not have endured the same misfortunes because he would have served the enlightened emperor Marcus Aurelius (AD 121–80), another figure we have already encountered. A member of the Antonine house, Marcus spent much of his reign (AD 161–80) in battle, defending the Empire from the barbarians across the Alps. He died, as they say, with his boots on, during a military campaign near Vienna. The Emperor's personal life was marred by adversity, including recurring illness, the loss of his father during his childhood, the premature death of most of his children and rumours of his wife Faustina's infidelity. Yet the nearly two decades of his rule were idealised as a golden age: a time when philosophers really did become kings, and with wisdom governed the commonweal. The idealisation began early, during the intensely unpopular rule of his son and successor, Commodus. The twelve-year reign of cruelty and corruption ended only when Commodus, the hateful son of a heroic father, was assassinated.

As the philosopher-king incarnate, Marcus took seriously the responsibilities of government, to the point of sulking about it. Struggling to live in accordance with philosophical principles, he recorded his beliefs (and his confessions and his self-reproaches) in a private little book that we now call the *Meditations*. The book is not a formal treatise, a doctrinal statement or even a loose collection of philosophical precepts. It is, rather, an intellectual diary: a gathering up of thoughts at the end of each day, however long, wearying or bloody the day had been. The prose is brief and terse throughout, as if Marcus were writing in the margins of his time. Which, in view of his weighty political and military responsibilities, was certainly the case. Although his commitment to austere self-examination was hardly idiosyncratic (it was, in fact, the very method recommended by Epictetus, whose writings Marcus had carefully studied), it resulted in a deeply personal document of one man's struggle to live virtuously, and thus happily.

Stoicism appears in the *Meditations* not as an unattainable goal but as a way of feeling at home in the world. Marcus, like his contemporaries, was concerned less with the idealised vision of the Stoic sage (so ideal that no one could live up to it) than with the daily grind of being a good person. The Stoic unflinchingly surveys the trials and tribulations of his life, but always from the standpoint of a dogged confidence in the universe's fundamental coherence, rationality and purpose. His constant conviction was that through sheer willpower (*vivere militare!*) he could move beyond unbridled desire to serene detachment. And so Marcus commanded himself to 'wrestle' to become the sort of man that 'Philosophy' wished him to be.[13] Happiness feels like wrestling not because it requires opponents to be defeated (in fact, there are no opponents because happiness lies within each person), but because it requires *us* to be ready and vigilant.

That the *Meditations* is one of the great bestsellers of Western philosophy is doubtless because Marcus was not a philosopher. But he was someone who wrote an intimate account of how philosophy could be a guide to right conduct. In keeping with the Stoic virtue of indifference, the *Meditations* is largely untroubled by contemporary events and incidents, a feature which also accounts for its timeless appeal. It was as if Marcus banished mundanities from his mind and raised the level of his attention to the larger questions of how life can be worthy and good. He pitched his thoughts perfectly: high enough to transcend everyday concerns, but not so high that he became (or we become) lost in abstractions. Marcus' words heal the worries and anxieties that beset not just himself, eighteen centuries ago, but also the readers beyond number who have profited, and do profit, from his practical wisdom.

Sweat, dirt and grease

Blaise Pascal, the seventeenth-century French philosopher and mathematician, declared, in a withering critique, that the Stoic knows the grandeur of mankind but not its humanity. Perhaps the French *savant* was thinking of Epictetus' brutally cynical remark that a new love affair is like a crystal wine glass: it's only a matter of time before it shatters. Beyond question, the Stoic code of behaviour is harsh and austere; mere mortals find it nearly impossible to uphold such exacting standards of constancy. For those of us who have not yet climbed wisdom's steep and winding path, or have failed in the attempt, Stoic values will not necessarily make things easier.

Like some parent impossible to please, Stoicism refuses to accept that failure, too, plays a role in the drama of humanity; that failure is part of what makes us human. It refuses any acknowledgement that pain and suffering are not merely hardships to be endured but, more crucially, experiences that might teach us about life's nature and purpose. (The Book of Job, coming up in the next chapter, has something to say on the matter.) Yes, the Stoic reaps the incontestable benefits of standing firm in adversity. Come what may, he endures; and endurance is a marvel to behold. But in between all that hardening and toughening we might lose sympathy for fellow travellers and become incapable of fathoming the depth of our own feelings. Tenacity, as Pascal understood, comes at a great price; a rock, for all its strength, is just a rock.

So here we must confront Stoicism's dark side: its contempt for the flesh-and-blood aspects of life. Such distaste for living in the world accounts for the uncomfortably morbid demeanour of many Stoic writers, and no one surpasses Marcus Aurelius for ruminating on the world's irreversible slide into decay and death: 'some things are hastening to be, others to have come and gone, and a part of what is coming into being is already extinct'.[14] As Marcus knew, the passage of time brings ever closer the moment not of our dignity but our demise. To use the language of science, the world is governed by the law of entropy: everything runs down, moving into disorder and eventual collapse.

Marcus' aversion to the natural shape of everyday life made for some disagreeable analogies. He exhorts himself to remember, in the very moment of sexual bliss, that his body is nothing but a carcass, whose destiny is to rot away. Forcing home the classic Stoic point that happiness does not depend upon external things, he judges that 'as your bath appears to your senses – soap, sweat, dirt, greasy water, all disgusting – so is every piece of life and every object'.[15] No doubt Marcus' bathwater was disgusting (especially after a day on the battle-field), but it takes a profound alienation from your own body to believe that the best image for life is dirt and grease and stink. Not surprisingly, Marcus retreats into the pristine fortress of his own mind, where he can put himself safely beyond the reach of bodily injury, worldly misfortune and bathtub scum.[16]

Other people's bodies could be equally foul. Unlike his subjects, Marcus did not enjoy the gladiatorial combats performed in amphi-theatres. (No doubt he preferred the real thing, where honour was to be gained on the true field of battle.) So distasteful did he find blood sports – he complained they made him nauseous – that he preferred during the contests to read his mail. The thousands of Romans gathered in the Coliseum for the excitement and brutality of the games could not have failed to witness Marcus' overt performance of Stoic indifference. No secret did the Emperor make of his reluctance to witness the atrocities that passed for public entertainment; duty alone explained his presence. He ordered gladiators to fight with blunted points on their spears and dulled blades on their swords, much to the dismay of bloodthirsty audiences who, through their shouts and roars, demanded that any gladiator who had not put up a good fight be killed on the spot. The crowds may have been insulted that their emperor showed more interest in state documents than the well-matched combatants in the arena below, but Marcus remained implacable in the face of their displeasure. He did not require 'the praise of the multitude' to make him happy.[17] No Stoic ever does.

8

The Hidden Face of God
(Judaism)

About twenty-five hundred years ago (although not even the scholars can settle on the date), a Hebrew poet turned an old story about a Bedouin sheik into a paean to suffering so majestically powerful that still today we stand in awe of its radical wisdom. We do not know who wrote the Book of Job, or when or where. If there were several authors, their hands have left no trace. To say that the poet (or poets) lived in the ancient Near East, somewhere between the Persian Gulf and the shores of the Nile, does not much help the matter. For the story is set in the lost land of Uz, and it refers to none of the major events in the history of the Israelites: the call of Abraham, the Exodus from Egypt or the captivity in Babylon. Nor can we be sure that Job himself is a Hebrew, for he says nothing about the Kings of Israel or the prophets and their teachings. Yet he is no pagan, either: he contends with the one God, the creator of heaven and earth.

With no historical clues to guide us, we must see Job as a solitary figure, stripped of mere locality; he is beholden to no one creed, attached to no single tribe, stands for no particular man. Rather, he stands for every man. In him we recognise the agonising truth of suffering that marks every human life. For who among us has not felt what Job has felt and demanded as he demanded to know the answer to the riddle of suffering? Whoever the Job-poet was, he was someone who had a conception of what suffering means – the pain, the misery, the lonely burdens, the unanswered sorrowful cries and the senseless ruin of it all. He must have lived in a world where injustice ran free, trampling goodness under its heavy foot; and he would not be surprised to know that, sadly, ours is much the same.

In the days before misfortune shadowed his life, Job was pious, upright and feared his God. There was no cause for that God to punish his faithful servant, and yet he chose, almost on a whim, to do just that. The story begins as Satan, that mischief-maker of old, insinuates that Job is virtuous only because he is prosperous; that his faith would retreat at misery's first attack. God confidently accepts the wager, and tests Job's loyalty – by ruining his life. First, his possessions are stolen. Which is nothing compared to what follows: his children are killed, crushed by the weight of the family home as it collapses in a tornado. Then affliction strikes the man himself, when oozing sores and scaly lesions cover his skin. Tortured, Job sits in the smouldering embers of what had been his home and scratches his cankerous flesh with a pottery shard retrieved from the rubble.

In his abject misery, he is visited by three friends: Eliphaz, Bildad and Zophar. As a mark of respect for Job's suffering, they sit with him in silence for seven days. But when they do speak, these men are fiercely critical – these men who should have sustained their friend with sympathy and love. In ever more menacing tones, they tell Job that he suffers because he has been wicked (even if no one can say exactly how), and that God always punishes the wicked just as he always rewards the virtuous. This is old theology, a spouted piety: man reaps as he sows. If only Job would repent his sins, then his misery would cease. 'But I have not sinned!' Job protests. He knows that he is a good man, and better than most. 'I hold fast to my righteousness and will not let go. My heart has not blasphemed all my days'. Blameless to the last, he does not deserve the affliction that God has sent him. So why did God send it? The answer remains hidden.

Suddenly, a new character bursts on to the scene: Elihu, the angry young man – angry that Job thinks himself more righteous than God and angry that Eliphaz, Bildad and Zophar have not answered Job's question. Though forceful in speech, this young hothead comes across no better than the venerable elders for whom he shows nothing but contempt. Not yet has Job been answered.

What makes Job such a modern (or is it timeless?) character is that he is a sceptical, restless and even rebellious soul. Though he encounters the world as a place of waste and suffering, still he believes in the goodness and perfection of his God. Cursed though he is by hard injustice, he does not dismiss life as meaningless but hungrily searches for its meaning. When he cannot find it, he demands – and yet how poorly that word conveys Job's fist-shaking impatience – that God reveal the meaning to him. Never does Job contemplate suicide, for he seeks not escape from life but life's fulfilment. Others might succumb to despair, and quickly so; but Job insists that life is always and unconditionally meaningful, even in the wretched here and the awful now. Here on the dung heap and now in the moment of misery.

Such is Job's sublimely human stance. The world is good because a good God created it. And it is in human existence that the creator's goodness is most plentifully manifest, for we *can* question him – and he *will* answer us. There is no reason, then, for goodness to be absent from life at any moment. Job does not want, nor does he expect, to postpone the satisfactions of life until the promised afterlife. True, he mourns his loss – 'my flesh is clad in worms and dust' – for he is only human; but he believes throughout that joy and goodness would also come his way: 'I hoped for good, but evil came./ I looked for light, but gloom came'. Job's steadfastness – to look for light in the midst of gloom – tells us that it is not right that man should find only evil and be covered only in darkness. God did not create this world for us to despise it and to long for release from its vale of tears. The world exists, rather, that we might find some fulfilment in it (even if our faith tells us that the greatest fulfilment lies in the hereafter). As surely as we are called to endure suffering in this life, we are invited to enjoy happiness. And in a way that seems hardly possible, suffering is what readies us for happiness.

Emboldened by righteousness, Job decides that God must be put on trial and held accountable for the suffering that with wanton cruelty he has inflicted upon an innocent humanity. God is the shaper of man but also man's downfall and his ruin, Job charges. 'Your hands shaped me and fashioned me/ Only to destroy me totally'. Audaciously, he will prosecute the case himself, for he demands nothing less than the right to challenge God to his face: 'I would press my suit to his face'. God, in turn, must show evidence of Job's guilt or admit that he is blameless and has suffered without cause – in which case God himself is guilty of a horrible injustice. Call it bravery, call it bluster, but it is no modest wish to put God in the witness stand. Yet it is Job's wish, and he does not shrink from it.

God, however, does seem to shrink from it, for he is nowhere to be found. 'Why do you hide your face?', Job beseeches. The divine suspect, who is also the divine judge, is on the run, a fugitive from himself:

Behold, if I go east – he is not there;
West – I do not discern him;
North – in his concealment I cannot behold him;
South – he is hidden and I cannot see him.

There is something beyond mere accusation in Job's words, for they are taunting. God must face the facts, or the facts will condemn him; condemn him as the weak God who cannot overthrow evil, or the cruel God who will not. As long as God hides his face, the problem of suffering cannot be solved. Job finally forces a confrontation with his mysterious persecutor. In defiant mood, he *will* have his answer.

Out of the whirlwind, it comes. At last God raises his voice, shows his face and gives his answer. But he gives it on *his* terms, not Job's. He does not answer the complaint – the wager with Satan and the horrible injustice done to Job are simply forgotten – but rather challenges the challenger. (The evasion is not for lack of words: this is God's longest speech in the Hebrew Bible.) In an abrupt reversal, it is man who stands trial for doubting God's governance of the world. It is the questioner who now must search out the answer. With the sting of a lash comes the humiliating charge, 'Where were *you* when I laid the earth's foundations?'. The force of it flattens Job, who confesses, 'Behold I am small; how can I refute you?'.

Yet Job is not completely vanquished, for he admits only his ignorance; the ignorance that he shares with every other child of Adam. Though he has been chastised for presuming to know more than his maker – how can the creature judge the creator? – he has not been branded a sinner. Despite the uncharitable presumption of Job's so-called friends, there is no sin to brand him. And so in the story's epilogue, God restores – nay, multiplies – Job's fortunes, sending him twice the number of sons lost and daughters more beautiful than before. He lives on happily for another one hundred and forty years, more blessed than he ever imagined he might be.

The wheel turns one last time, only Job does not know it. God remembers his moral courage, and praises his faithful servant for having 'spoken the truth'. And that is why God sides with Job: because he alone found the strength to contend with God; to wrestle with life's perplexities and penetrate its secrets. Job does not know that the wheel has turned, but we do. We know the last triumphant truth of his bitter agony: that it is right to demand more and better from the world; right to seek meaning in life as it comes to us; and right to expect happiness in the midst of suffering.

In the story of Job we find an almost cosmic definition of happiness, one more abstract than we have seen and one far removed from any simplistic notion that happiness has anything to do with pleasure or good fortune. Through this parable of suffering we see happiness in an unaccustomed light – as bound up in our search for the meaning of life when life seems most meaningless. In some sense, happiness *is* the search for meaning against all odds. Which is why suffering is no barrier to happiness but a means – so improbable, so unwelcome – for discovering just what happiness is.

Freely imperfect

The Talmud, the rabbinical commentary on the Hebrew Bible that has been developed and studied over centuries, speaks of God's humility in creation. God deliberately curtailed his powers and allowed himself to call into being the poor imperfect substance known as man. Our imperfections – causing harm, doing wrong, making others suffer – mark us out as God's fallible creatures. When he could have done otherwise, God limited his unbounded goodness to create within us the possibility of evil. Our most damning flaw is the surest sign of our humanity. Animals are ferocious but not evil; nor do the angels risk villainy. Only mankind sins.

But in no way should we cultivate that flaw, as the rabbis instruct. The rosebush bears thorns, but that does not mean we should prick ourselves on them. Better that we do not. Evil exists in somewhat the same way: so that we might avoid it. If evil possesses a value, it is never a 'face value' but only a submerged one. We cannot find any forthright merit in something so senseless, so irrational, as evil. And yet we might find merit half hidden. If we must credit evil, then let us credit it as the price to be paid for knowing – and doing – what is right and what is good.

In *Faith after the Holocaust* (1973), the Jewish philosopher Eliezer Berkovits (1908–92) maintains that without evil there can be no good, for each presupposes the other in the way that contrary things always do. Just as we know light as the opposite of darkness, we know good as evil's opposite. If vice were not a possibility then virtue would not be an actuality, for what is virtue but the conscious rejection of vice? Evil exists so that we may spurn it, and in that spurning know ourselves as inherently moral beings; as beings capable of creating happiness in their lives by filling it with virtue.

But virtue, as Berkovits reminds us, must be freely chosen, because our choosing is what matters. To be virtuous under compulsion — you would like to shoplift, but you don't because the closed circuit television camera would expose you — is not to be virtuous but only obedient. Virtue arises only when you *could* do something wrong, and then do not. (This is why surveillance is dehumanising: it robs us of our basic freedom to choose right over wrong.) Our freedom to choose good over evil depends, as Berkovits insists, upon our own imperfection. Perfection is 'unfree' because it cannot deviate from itself, lest it become imperfect. Only imperfect things can change, and for that very reason only they are free.

Though it seems incredible, our freedom rests upon our failure. For it is only when the gap is exposed between the world as it is and as it might be that we are spurred on to make decisions and take action. The world and its people are not entirely good; but they can become better — or worse. And so the hope for our improvement is also the threat of decay, for at any moment the world can either climb upward or spiral down. Such is the awesome responsibility of human freedom.

God's unspeakable silence

The question of suffering arouses fiery passions and enraged accusations against God. The question is never answered, but the passions are cooled and the questioner finds at last some peace. Job's peace was not that God answered him (he did not), but that he was *present* to him. God came out of hiding and made himself known to the challenger. 'I have heard of you with my ears/ But now my eyes see you'. And that was enough for Job, who, despite the troubles and trials heaped upon him, never faltered in his faith. It was the very power that drove his accusations against God. If Job had renounced his faith, he would not have bothered with God, since to him God would be dead. Despite the understandably angry urgings of his wife, Job did not abandon his god, even though it seemed that his god had abandoned him.

God also abandoned the six million in the death camps. He did not appear to them, despite *their* challenges and *their* belief against all odds. He did not intervene in that dark moment of history to save the Jews or the gypsies or the homosexuals or all the other innocent victims of the Nazis' murderous fury. No, they were left desolate in their misery, to extract meaning, if somehow they could, from suffering and despair. This tragedy did not end in the way that art and literature tell us it should have ended: with God's last-minute appearance to right all wrongs and restore the world's moral order. In this twentieth-century tragedy, God remained off-stage. Not like a prompter, helpfully feeding the actors their cues. But blank and mute. God's silence feels to us like a punishment: his tacit permission that evil should pollute and corrupt our world. In our anger and confusion, we cannot help but ask, 'Where was God when the millions were murdered?' We cannot help but ask.

Yet we cannot hope to be answered. As Berkovits believed, the question 'Where was God in Auschwitz?' is unanswerable because it arises from a mistaken premise. Our mistake is to presume that God will manifest himself in human history in just the way we want him to. Job fell into the same trap, insisting that God conform to his own expectations and bend his divine shape to a merely human will. Proudly, we demand a god of our own devising – one who is forever ready to protect his faithful servants and subdue their enemies. But history mocks our expectation that God should work to our schedule and not his own. The Holocaust, genocide in Rwanda, the attack on the World Trade Center – these are but a few examples of thousands that could be named – tell us that God presents himself in history mostly as the uninvolved bystander, the silent witness to abomination.

But why was God silent? If he wished, he could intervene in history at any moment to punish the guilty. But that would turn the world into a kind of prison, for we would live in constant fear of punishment. Like a puppet that moves only on command, we would obey God only under coercion, and thus perform an illusion of freedom. But we were not created to be puppets, and it is ludicrous to speak of a puppet's happiness. We were created to be free, and to use our freedom to forge our happiness.

It is to safeguard our necessary freedom, the Jewish philosophers have taught, that God shows his presence in history more by restraint than strength. Like a parent who shows forbearance to a misbehaving child, God displays through his inaction strength beyond brute force. He willingly casts himself into shackles and renders himself powerless in the face of evil so that our dignity can be preserved and our freedom guaranteed. In Berkovits's arresting metaphor, God cannot 'bludgeon' mankind into goodness.[1] So instead of asking 'Why is God silent?', let us ask 'What happens to us in God's silence?' One answer is that he preserves the possibility of our creating meaning and purpose in the world even in its most despairing moments, and so gives us the chance of working towards happiness. Not a happiness that entails pleasure or the satisfaction of desire, but one that makes us authentically alive, more real than we have ever been.

Why sleepest thou, O Lord?

Although it resonates deeply for the generations that struggle to keep their faith after Auschwitz, the Talmudic doctrine of *hester panim* – 'the hiding of the face' – dates from biblical times. We remember Job's mournful cry of divine injustice, 'Why do you hide your face?'. The prophet Isaiah calls God *El Mistater*, the hidden God: 'Verily thou art a God that hidest thyself, God of Israel, Saviour'. It is crucial, though, that for Isaiah the hidden God is a *saving* God not a cruel one. The Psalmist, too, wrote of that grievous moment when God, made sorrowful by the cruelty of his creation, looked the other way:

Awake, why sleepest thou, O Lord?
Arise, cast us not off for ever.
Wherefore hidest thou thy face,

> And forgettest our affliction and our oppression?
> For our soul is bowed down to the dust:
> Our belly cleaveth unto the earth.
> Arise for our help,
> And redeem us for thy mercies' sake.

We might, if we are believers, feel within us the same anguish at God's absence; we might share the poet's lament that our creator is blind to our suffering and deaf to our pleas for redemption and mercy.

Another Psalm speaks our suffering more plaintively: 'How long, O Lord, wilt thou forget me, for ever?/ How long wilt thou hide thy face from me?'. The suffering stretches out for all time, and the Psalmist fears that God will be always hidden, always unmindful of his creation. Not if we waited a lifetime, nor a lifetime of lifetimes, would he turn his face towards us. It is hard to say what is more striking about the Psalms: God's silence or man's noisy refusal of it. In the silence that fosters not tranquillity but only anxiety, we still long for God's redeeming presence. How in that silence can we ever hear his voice?

What the rabbis propose stretches all credulity: that God's silence is the symbol not of his absence – but his *presence*. Like a child playing 'hide-and-seek' (to venture an impertinent simile), God is still present but out of sight and waiting to be found. Although we are unaware of him, he is still *there* – 'in the game' – like the child crouched underneath the table or lurking behind the chair. Of course the analogy quickly finds its limit, for we do not experience God's absence in anything like a playful spirit. It comes upon us, rather, as the distress of abandonment and the torture of doubt. We look and look for a sign of the Creator's loving presence, and from here to the horizon's far edge we find nothing at all.

Why does God hide? Not because we force him, for mankind cannot compel the almighty. God's indifference is not a disapproving judgement upon us, not a punishment or sign of his anger. It is, rather, part of his divine nature: he is the God who hides. And he hides for a reason that we have come upon again and again – our freedom. To be good we must choose to be so; but to choose, we must be free. Without freedom there is no authentic choice but only compulsion (like the puppet jerked on the string). If God's presence in history were convincing – fully manifest, never in doubt, always on show – it would sabotage our freedom. God *must* be hidden as mankind goes about its work so that it might do so responsibly. By necessity, then, our freedom carries the risk of evil, and it cannot be pre-ordained that the risk will be avoided. God will not stop us from being bad if that is our choice; he will not reach down, grab us by the collar and hold us back just as we are about to harm another. Malice is as much an expression of our freedom as generosity. It's just not an expression that does us credit.

Through the gift of freedom, God gives us scope to be human. Although he hopes that we use the gift wisely, he knows that we might not. And so he waits. As God waits for goodness to shine through, the world descends into evil. The wicked prosper and the violent conquer and the oppressors triumph. There is no alternative, and there is no cause to regret it. For man to be man he must be free to choose evil; for God to be God he must grant the choice.

Such is the moral contradiction of our world. God denies his essence, allowing the world to be imperfect when he could have made it perfect and scarcely noticed the trouble he had taken. So that goodness may triumph – if not today, then a joyful someday – he permits the scourge of evil. When evil does rise up in the world, God hides his face as the sign that he accepts such a baleful necessity. As the Psalms so movingly express, the paradox of divine existence is that God, to show his love, abandons some of us to a fate so heartless that we experience it as brutal indifference to our blameless suffering. True, God could eliminate suffering, for he can do anything. But then he would have to eliminate mankind – and return the world to its original nothingness – for there is no such thing as a humanity that does not suffer. Not because we are guilty, but because suffering is our lot. Job is entitled to be angry at his misfortune; but he is not entitled to be angry with his God, for God is not misfortune's cause.

In our life we may come to know what Job knew: that the problem of evil can *never* be answered in a way that will satisfy us. We cannot make sense of bad things for there is nothing comprehensible about them. Not everything happens for a good reason, although we wish that were true – and so often we are told it *is* true – because at least that would give us comfort when comfort is most needed. But the hard truth is that the wound of suffering pains us deeply, no matter how cleverly we theorise our dilemma; no matter how artfully we try to explain it away. In the face of our distress, God is silent – the voice that spoke to Job out of a whirlwind did not answer the charge of injustice; did not even admit that injustice had been done. But, with an insistence to rival Job's, we may ask not why God is silent, but what happens in that silence. And like Job, we shall be answered.

Our answer comes in the voice of tradition, a voice telling us that the mystery of God's silence is explained by the change that overcomes *us* in the silence. That, too, is what Job discovered: we are changed – and possibly for the better, though of that there can be no guarantee – by circumstances not of our approval, let alone our design. We cannot expect that suffering's harshness will fade away, for its causes (mere accident, malicious intent) will always be found in our world. Yet we can expect, or hope at least, that suffering will bring about a change within us.

We can use our inner freedom – the freedom that never shall be overthrown – to choose how we bear our burdens, intolerable though they seem. That choice is more than Stoic endurance, for it aims at something that surpasses mere peace of mind. In the ruins of suffering, in the blank unreasonableness of it all, we can strive to build up a meaning to life and thus cling to happiness. Never because of suffering but only in its spite; for always we wish that the opportunity had never come along. Like the desert patriarch in the ancient lost land of Uz, we can choose to be worthy of our trials and our torments, finding a meaning to life in the midst of our suffering; a meaning that no punishing darkness can ever extinguish.

Worthy of our suffering

This is no empty proverb, detached from worldly concerns or untested in the crucible of hard experience. It is a perennial truth ever to be discovered anew, and so it was found again in the grim time of the Holocaust. The systematic annihilation of European Jewry in the Nazi death camps stands as a perverse monument to pure evil. As such, it has raised questions not only about Judaism itself but about the future of humanity. The horror of the Holocaust has made us realise that our 'age of reason' has not put an end to barbarism. But it has also made us realise that within us survives the need for fulfilment beyond expectation. Sixty years on, the Holocaust demands that we continue to resist evil – by having hope for the world.

In his classic memoir *Man's Search for Meaning*, the famed Viennese psychotherapist Viktor Frankl (1905–97) – himself a survivor of Auschwitz – wrote that in any circumstance, no matter how dire, man retains his spiritual freedom: an independence of mind and soul, even when the body is bound and fettered by uncontrollable forces. 'We who lived in the concentration camps,' Frankl recalled,

> can remember the men who walked through the huts comforting oth-
> ers, giving away their last piece of bread. They may have been few in
> number, but they offer sufficient proof that everything can be taken
> from a man but one thing: the last of the human freedoms – to choose
> one's attitude in any given set of circumstances, to choose one's own
> way.[2]

These are inspiring words (and ones that call to mind the heroism of Seneca, Cicero and all the other Roman Stoics), for they help us to see how suffering can be a proud achievement. Not, to be sure, one that we seek out – there is no merit in needless suffering, let us continue to be clear about that – but one that steals upon us in the course of life. In desolate circumstances, when we are denied all possibility of positive action, when we can change nothing – nothing except ourselves – our sole achievement may be to endure our sufferings honourably. *How* we accept an unavoidable fate, *how* we shoulder our burdens, is what makes all the difference. The decision to endure is freedom's last stand: the final chance, as Dostoevsky put it, to be 'worthy of our suffering'.

What a noble sentiment! But perhaps fraudulent, too. What does it mean to suffer worthily? It means, first of all, a stubborn refusal to be defined and determined by circumstance alone. We are not hostages to fortune, though fortune (be it good or bad) will have its due. Rarely can we decide what shall happen to us; but always we decide what shall *become of us*. That is so, Frankl explains, because the sort of person we wish to become rests upon an 'inner decision', one that need not be forfeited in the face of adversity. As the deaths of the martyrs in the concentration camps testify, there is a hallowed dignity even in life's final wretched moments. Despair is the wrong conclusion to be drawn from the unalterable fact of suffering, for that is to concede that our response is likewise unalterable.

Yet there is a still higher meaning to the worthiness of suffering than moral courage. Our inner convictions – our anchor in a sea of troubles – must arise from somewhere. And that somewhere is the uniquely human recognition that, as Frankl puts it, we live *sub specie aeternitatis*, under the aspect of the eternal. Our life is never entirely what it seems to be right now (and thus never fully perceptible at any one instant) because life is always provisional; always unfolding in the light of larger, ultimate concerns. It is part of man's nature to understand that the source of his inner strength is embracing a future goal, be it a particular action, a certain kind of relationship, or a distinctive experience.

We must have a future to live *for*, and so we always live partly in anticipation – which, of course, can be either hopeful or despairing. Being fully human is never about brute animalistic survival but always about living for something, or someone, other than ourselves. Life's fulfilment lies in our attachment to what transcends immediate experience and what rises above the concerns of today. Which is why, as Frankl explains, we willingly put on the yoke of suffering – but only on the condition that our suffering has a meaning. Or rather that it lets us forge a meaning. Our suffering is not punishment for our sins; not a lesson in humility; not a test of endurance; and not a mystery beyond comprehension. Suffering, in all its irrationality, all its senselessness, is life's call to us – the call to re-examine our false ideas about happiness; the call to witness the truth of our being.

Though he arrives at his conclusion in a specifically Jewish context, Frankl makes what he believes to be a general point. Indeed, he claims that the drive to find meaning – the 'will to meaning', as he calls it – motivates every human life. The drive expresses itself, and healthily so, as a tension: the painful recognition of the gap between our life as it is and as it might be. Mistakenly, we presume that the blessed life is the carefree one, when no pressures bear down upon us and no challenges rudely rise up. Such is the near-catatonic state promoted by the modern pharmaceutical industry as the lifestyle of choice. But a life so static can scarcely be called human, for it lacks the propulsion of *futurity* that only humans possess: the galvanising awareness that we live not just for today but for a tomorrow that we strive to make better. To worry that our life is not yet good enough is to be in a very healthy state of mind – one conducive to moral growth – even though in the moment we feel only distress. We are longing to be answerable for our own lives; longing to be worthy of life itself. Longing to be happy.

Here, again, we remember Job, who thought that the solution to the riddle of life's meaning was to accuse God of injustice. Yet what happened was that life's meaning was thrown back upon him with a nearly crushing force, and he understood that the universe was not answerable to him, but he to it. '*I* will ask questions and *you* will inform me,' Yahweh commanded in a voice that carries on the wind across the millennia. Although it would be marvellous indeed if we could learn the lesson some easier and gentler way (usually, we learn it through suffering), life is mostly about the questions that it asks of us, the demands it places upon us, and the worthiness of our response to its commanding call. 'What does life expect of me?' – *that* is the question to ask in the moment of suffering.

Happiness is what happens as we search for meaning in circum-stances of such bewilderment and perplexity that they appear to render meaning absurd. Happiness is less the meaning itself than the quest for it, the conscious orientation of our lives towards a future goal and a fuller purpose. So we might say that we do not create meaning in life so much as discover it. The meaning is there all the time, implicit, undeclared, and waiting patiently until we are ready to listen. But we find it hard to listen because we would rather be doing the speaking. We would rather be God than Job. So hard is it for us to listen that sometimes it takes the shock and roar of a whirlwind to silence us.

The fire within

If there is meaning in the totality of life, there is meaning in suffering, for it is as much a part of life's charted course as birth and death. Neither invited nor welcome, and to be avoided whenever it can be, suffering is, nonetheless, part of what makes a life full and complete. To live as if suffering were an affront to our humanity and a barrier to our happiness is to miss the point of what it means to be human and happy.

In *With God in Hell*, his account of heroism and enduring faith in the Jewish ghettos and death camps, Berkovits recounts a story of happiness in the face of suffering. A group of young Hasidic men from Plaszow, a concentration camp just outside Krakow, were forced to jump into a pit that would become their mass grave. They knew that German soldiers would fire upon them as they fell, so that if suffocation did not kill them the machine guns would. '[A]s if a fire had been lit within them', the Hasidim began 'to sing and dance'.[3] Oblivious to the armed soldiers, the young men danced their way to death as the spray of bullets hit their twisting bodies in mid air. They imposed another rhythm, as it were, upon their suffering; they remade their reality by setting down order on the chaos of experience. Through rebellion, they denied another, seemingly more powerful, reality.

Berkovits believed (although he was not there) that in their final moments the innocent victims 'lived their lives as Jews with an intensity and meaningfulness never before experienced'.[4] Should we be shocked that he called this tragic episode a moment of supreme happiness? Is that not a gross moral imposture, turning something intrinsically evil into an unwitting good? Yet the moment's profound authenticity depended upon the soldiers who did not hesitate to open fire; it could not have been otherwise. Those young men sanctified their lives in life's last moment, creating holiness in the midst of abomination. They found a happiness that delivered them from fear, and did not forsake them in the hour of greatest peril. Scandalously, the price of their happiness was the reality of evil.

The reality of evil and the fact of suffering are the price of everyone's happiness. Which is the lesson of the Holocaust and the lesson of the Book of Job: to live the kind of life you choose in the face of circumstances *never* of your choosing. And yet is there really an alternative? The essence of one's being does not wait for a more congenial setting, a more propitious moment, a better time.

Conclusion

Since so much of our time in this book has been spent simply trying to understand the scope and scale of happiness, it would be negligent, in this concluding moment, not to shift our attention from the 'seeking' to the 'finding'. Without in any way pretending to offer the last word on the matter, I'd like to end by describing, all too briefly, what it might mean to find happiness. Of course to put it that way is to overstate the case, to make it more of a departure than it actually is, for in truth we have been anticipating this moment all along. The insights expressed in these final pages have been gradually gathering force. If the lives of Epicurus, Seneca and Ghazali, the stories of Buddha and Prince Arjuna, and the mystery of Job tell us anything, they tell us that the seeking of happiness flows into the finding of it, just as the rushing waters of a river pour out effortlessly into the calm ocean depth, and so cease to rush.

The relief of being ordinary

For me, the most liberating insight about our pursuit of happiness, liberating because it helps us to overcome so many threatening anxieties, is that we do not have to become someone else to be happy. In a way, this truth is trivial: how can we be other than who we are? But what is far from trivial is the disturbing and all too prevalent belief that to find happiness we must turn our backs on all that is familiar, forge a new life, journey to distant lands, perform extraordinary acts, exchange a dismal present for a fantastic future, or wish upon an auspicious star.

Such efforts are wasteful because they squander the opportunity that is always before us: to become not someone else – that is the perverted goal of the 'makeover' ethos – but a better version of the person we already are. Whoever we are, and whatever circumstances we face – and for nearly all of us, they will be ordinary ones – the possibility of happiness always surrounds us. We are always in the right place, though we do our best to forget it.

This theme of accepting our ordinariness appears in so many versions of happiness. In Seneca's insistence that we do not need any 'great equipment' to be happy. In *The Conference of the Birds*, when, after a long and hazardous journey, the birds discover that they are their own true king. In the practicality of *karma yoga*. Perhaps even in the silence of Thomas Aquinas we might hear a hymn of contentment.

So let us cultivate a happiness that is authentically ours and let us be happy with the things that will make us so. To be authentically happy means to take possession of ourselves, to bring about the person we are in potential, to become *more real*. As Voltaire famously put it, 'We must make our garden grow.' Action is the heart of an authentic existence because only in action do we attain fulfilment. Of course 'action' is not just striking out in the world but a directed realisation of the kind of person we imagine ourselves to be. In that way, we give our lives a coherent shape, and rescue ourselves from dissolution and waste. Through purposeful action, we *become* our future and find our contentment. We accomplish ourselves. Is it too much, too paradoxical, to say that happiness feels like growing up? We make happiness as best we can within life as it is, and do not import it from some magical elsewhere.

The homecoming of happiness

To search for happiness is not to embark upon a voyage to an exotic distant land, but to return home. Whether actual or symbolic, the homecoming is a common feature in many different stories about the quest for happiness. Ghazali returned to his birthplace in Persia after spending years in prayerful solitude in foreign lands. Viveka was restored to his royal home. Prince Arjuna decided not to forsake his kinsmen. The Buddha was born – and died – in a grove of sala trees. Though each story is distinctive they all reveal the general truth – the truth for all of us, no matter who, no matter where – that happiness must feel like something that we once knew, perhaps only dimly, but now are finding again, although this time with a greater resolve and a surer purpose. In a way, we are discovering a part of ourselves that we had never known.

Though self-help gurus, life coaches and other purveyors of self-esteem might tell us otherwise, becoming happy is not a kind of deliberate consumer choice. We do not appraise paths to happiness dispassionately, as if we were on the lookout for a bargain, ready to negotiate the best deal we can. In a way, the path finds *us*, for it must always fit the shape and size of life as we live it right here and right now. We end up with the only kind of happiness that we can: one that suits us, that feels right for us because it is 'in sync' with our life's rhythm and pace.

Within the span of our days

It is a cliché that the secret of happiness must come to us like a bolt out of the blue. It is also wrong. The secret must be an open one, otherwise it would defeat its very purpose, which is that we should know it. We are born to be happy, for happiness is the perfection of our existence. And we *can* achieve it. Not easily, and perhaps not on our own. And maybe there is yet more happiness in the life to come. But we forge a happiness in this life.

Only an evil genius would create us to be happy and then make the achieving of it so damnably hard that we give up in torment and despair. Happiness cannot take us entirely by surprise, cannot steal upon us, because it is an enterprise that requires our investment. For all its connotations of blissful epiphany, happiness is a rather pragmatic affair. It must must lie within our reach and fall within the span of our days.

Happiness for all

That we shall find happiness cannot be guaranteed. Which is another way of saying that, however much the 'desire industry' tries to persuade us otherwise, we are not entitled to be happy. We are entitled only to work for it. This entitlement we all share, simply because we are human. The chance for happiness is an irreducible part of our being, a part from which no one can be disqualified.

Yet for the pursuit of happiness to remain free and open, it cannot be contingent upon the acquisition of esoteric knowledge or the profession of certain beliefs. When the right to find happiness comes with conditions – 'Yes, you can be happy; but only if …' – it ceases to be a right: it becomes, instead, a privilege. And, like all privileges, its conferral (and repeal) depends upon someone else's authority. But we have only to be born to possess the right to make ourselves happy. It is a perversion of that right, and an offence against human dignity, to attach too many strings to the offer of happiness. So what matters is not that your pursuit of happiness is sanctioned by an authority figure (be it religious or secular) but that it works for you – that it actually *makes you happy*.

Bound to the world – and beyond

We cannot find happiness in isolation. A certain amount of quiet and calm reflection is surely necessary just to understand what happiness means, but the activity of *becoming happy* is one that binds us to the world. Finding happiness means not despising the world but wanting to create a better one within it. We might say, then, that our happiness is nested in the world, for the world is where, over a lifetime, we patiently build up the layers of a habitat – and the action of 'habit' is crucial here – that we can proudly call good.

Yet the happy life is also one of ideals, of symbols of something higher, greater, deeper and vaster than ourselves. It is a profoundly human need to aspire to something *more*, and to be carried by that aspiration beyond horizon's edge. We want to envision something that surpasses our selfish desires, that outstrips merely personal goals; and then we want to attain it. Of course from time to time we shall fail in that attainment, but we shall have learned enough to know that we are stronger than our failures. Our life is an ever striving, and we call the striving happiness.

Notes

Introduction

1. Richard Layard, *Happiness: Lessons from a New Science* (London: Allen Lane, 2005), p. 224.
2. Robert Biswas-Diener, Ed Diener and Maya Tamir, 'The psychology of subjective well-being', *Daedalus* (Spring 2004), p. 19.
3. Layard, *Happiness*, p. 12.
4. Biswas-Diener *et al.*, 'The psychology of subjective well-being', p. 18.
5. Richard A. Easterlin, 'The economics of happiness', *Daedalus* (Spring 2004) p. 26.
6. Ruut Veenhoven, *Conditions of Happiness* (D. Reidel Publishing Company: Dordecht, Holland, 1984), p. 18.
7. Seneca, *De Vita Beata* 8, in *Seneca: Four Dialogues*, ed. C.D.N. Costa (Warminster: Aris & Phillips, 1994).
8. Seneca, *Consolatio ad Helviam* 5, in *Seneca: Four Dialogues*, ed. C.D.N. Costa (Warminster: Aris & Phillips, 1994).
9. Robert Nozick, *The Examined Life: Philosophical Meditations* (New York: Simon and Schuster, 1989), pp. 99–117.
10. J.M. Keynes, 'Economic Possibilities for Our Grandchildren', *The Collected Writings of John Maynard Keynes*, vol. 9 (London: The Macmillan Press Ltd, 1972), pp. 321–32, quotation at p. 328.
11. Keynes, 'Economic Possibilities', pp. 329–30.

1. *Maximise Your Pleasure (The Utilitarians)*

1. Jeremy Bentham, *An Introduction to the Principles of Morals and Legislation*, ed. J.H. Burns and H.L.A. Hart (1791; Oxford University Press, 1996), Preface, p. 4.
2. Bentham, *IPML*, p. 12.
3. Bentham, *IPML*, p. 11.
4. Bentham, *IPML*, p. 11.
5. Bentham, *IPML*, p. 12.
6. Bentham, *IPML*, section 4, note; p. 38.
7. Bentham, *IPML*, 17.8; p. 285.
8. Bentham, *IPML*, 1.1; p. 74.
9. Quoted in V.J. McGill, *The Idea of Happiness* (New York: Frederick A. Praeger, 1967), p. 119.
10. J.S. Mill, *Autobiography of John Stuart Mill* (New York: Columbia University Press, 1924), p. 58.
11. Mill, *Autobiography*, p. 47.
12. Mill, *Autobiography*, p. 94.
13. Mill, *Autobiography*, p. 94.
14. Mill, *Autobiography*, p. 99.
15. Mill, *Autobiography*, p. 99.
16. Mill, *Autobiography*, p. 104.
17. Mill, *Autobiography*, p. 100.
18. Mill, *Autobiography*, p. 110.
19. Mill, *Autobiography*, p. 113.
20. J. M. Robson, *et al.*, eds., *Collected Works of John Stuart Mill*, 33 vols., (Toronto and London: University of Toronto Press, 1980–91), X, p. 96.
21. J.S. Mill, *Utilitarianism*, ed. Roger Crisp (1861; Oxford: Oxford University Press, 1998), 2.4.27–8; p. 56.
22. Mill, *Utilitarianism*, 2.4.29; p. 56
23. Mill, *Utilitarianism*, 2.6.18; p. 57.
24. Mill, *Utilitarianism*, 2.6.40–44; p. 57.
25. Mill, *Utilitarianism*, 2.15–16; p. 62.

26. Mill, *Utilitarianism*, 2.18.6; p. 64.
27. Mill, *Utilitarianism*, 2.18.6–9; p. 64.
28. Mill, *Utilitarianism*, 17.7; p. 64.

2. *Pleasure is Good (The Epicureans)*

1. Epicurus, *Letter to Menoeceus*, in Brad Inwood and L.P. Gerson, trans. and eds., *The Epicurus Reader: Selected Writings and Testiminia* (Cambridge: Hackett Publishing Co., 1994), p. 28.
2. Lucretius, *On the Nature of the Universe*, trans. R.E. Latham (London: Penguin Books, 1951), Book III, p. 96.
3. Epicurus, *Letter to Menoeceus*, p. 29.
4. Epicurus, *Letter to Menoeceus*, p. 30.
5. Epicurus, *Letter to Menoeceus*, p. 31.
6. Cicero, *De Finibus*, trans. and ed. H. Rackham (London: William Heinemann, 1914), Book I, p. 41.
7. Lucretius, *On the Nature of the Universe*, Book II, p. 60.

3. *Get Busy with Your Works (Hinduism)*

1. *Chandogya Upanishad*, in *A Source Book in Indian Philosophy*, eds. Sarvepalli Radhakrishnan and Charles A. Moore (Princeton: Princeton University Press, 1957), pp. 69–70.
2. Ramakrishna, *Works* (Mylapore, Madras: Sri Ramakrishna Math, 1922), 1: 222–3; quoted in Troy Wilson Organ, *The Hindu Quest for the Perfection of Man* (Athens, OH: Ohio University Press, 1970), p. 25.
3. *The Bhagavad Gita*, ed. R.C. Zaehner (London: Oxford University Press, 1966), 2.33, pp. 36–7.
4. Kim Kott, *Hinduism: A Very Short Introduction* (Oxford: Oxford University Press, 1998), p. 38.
5. Swami Vivekananda, *Bhakti-Yoga: The Yoga of Love and Devotion* (Calcutta: Advaita Ashrama, 1974), p. 31.

6. *Bhagavata Puranas* 2.3.20–24; quoted in David N. Lorenzen, 'Bhakti', in *The Hindu World*, eds. Sushil Mittal and Gene Thursby (London: Routledge, 2004), p. 194.

7. Swami Vivekananda, *Bhakti-Yoga*, p. 35.

8. *Bhakti Sutra* 44; quoted in Organ, *The Hindu Quest for the Perfection of Man*, p. 259.

4. The Enlightened One (Buddhism)

1. *The Dhammapada*, trans. Juan Mascaró (Harmondsworth: Penguin, 1973), p. 336.

2. Quoted in Vicki Mackenzie, ed., *Why Buddhism?: Westerners in Search of Wisdom* (London: Thorsons, 2003), p. 265.

3. *Why Buddhism?*, pp. 6–9.

4. *Why Buddhism?*, p. 9.

5. *Why Buddhism?*, pp. 259–60.

5. Only in Heaven (Christianity)

1. G.K. Chesterton, *St. Thomas Aquinas* (New York: Sheed & Ward, Inc., 1933), p. 71.

2. *Summa Theologiae*, Part 1 of Part 2, Question 5, Article 5. Thomas Aquinas, *Treatise on Happiness*, ed. and trans. John A. Oesterle (Notre Dame, IN: University of Notre Dame Press, 1983), p. 61.

3. *Summa Theologiae*, Part 1 of Part 2, Question 1, Article 5; trans. Oesterle, p. 10.

4. *Summa Theologiae*, Part 1 of Part 2, Question 3, Article 8; trans. Oesterle, p. 39.

5. Aquinas, *De Potentia*, Q.7, a.5, ad. 14; quoted in Karen Armstrong, *A History of God* (London: Vintage, 1999), p. 238.

6. *Summa Theologiae*, Part 1 of Part 2, Question 3, Article 2; trans. Oesterle, p. 30.

6. The Alchemy of Happiness (Islam)

1. Abu Hamid al-Ghazali, *The Deliverance from Evil*, in W. Montgomery Watt, *The Faith and Practice of Al-Ghazali* (London: George Allen and Unwin Ltd, 1953), p. 21.

2. *Deliverance from Evil*, in *Faith and Practice of Al-Ghazali*, p. 55.

3. *Deliverance from Evil*, in *Faith and Practice of Al-Ghazali*, p. 57.

4. *Deliverance from Evil*, in *Faith and Practice of Al-Ghazali*, p. 76.

5. Abu Hamid al-Ghazali, *The Alchemy of Happiness*, trans. and ed. Claud Field and Elton L. Daniel (London: M. E. Sharpe, Inc., 1991), p. 52.

6. Shabistari, *The Secret Rose Garden*, quoted in John Baldock, *The Essence of Sufism* (Royston: Eagle Editions Ltd, 2004), p. 202.

7. Fariduddin Attar, *The Conference of the Birds*, trans. C.S. Nott (London: Routledge & Kegan Paul, 1978), p. 219.

8. Jalal al-Din Rumi, quoted in Kenneth Cragg, ed. *The Wisdom of the Sufis* (New York: New Directions, 1976), p. 13.

9. Shabistari, *The Secret Rose Garden*, quoted in Baldock, *The Essence of Sufism*, p. 200.

7. It's All in Your Mind (The Stoics)

1. Cicero, *Tusculan Disputations*, trans. and ed. A.E. Douglas (Warminster: Aris & Phillips, 1990), Book 5, 12.

2. Cicero, *De Finibus*, trans. and ed. H. Rackham (London: William Heinemann, 1914), Book 3, 45.

3. *Tusculan Disputations*, Book 5, 27.79.

4. Seneca, *De Vita Beata* 2.3, in *Seneca: Four Dialogues*, ed. C.D.N. Costa (Warminster: Aris & Phillips, 1994).

5. *De Vita Beata* 10.

6. *De Vita Beata* 7.

7. *Tusculan Disputations*, Book 2, 4.1

8. Cicero, *On Divination*, Book 2, 1.1; in Cicero, *On the Good Life*, trans. and ed. Michael Grant (London: Penguin Books, 1971) p.3.

9. *Tusculan Disputations*, Book 5, 6.16.

10. Tacitus, *Annals of Imperial Rome*, trans. and ed. Michael Grant (1956; London: Penguin Books, 1989), Book 15, 62.

11. Seneca, *Consolatio ad Helviam* 5, in *Seneca: Four Dialogues*, ed. C.D.N. Costa (Warminster: Aris & Phillips, 1994).

12. *De Vita Beata* 4.

13. *The 'Meditations' of Marcus Aurelius Antoninus...*, ed. R.B. Rutherford, trans. A.S.L. Farquaharson and R.B. Rutherford (Oxford: Oxford University Press, 1989), 6.30.

14. *Meditations*, 6.15.

15. *Meditations*, 8.24.

16. *Meditations*, 8.48.

17. *Meditations*, 3.6.

8. *The Hidden Face of God (Judaism)*

1. Eliezer Berkovits, *Faith after the Holocaust* (New York: Ktav Publishing House Inc., 1973), p. 89.

2. Viktor E. Frankl, *Man's Search for Meaning* (1946; London: Random House, 2004), p. 75.

3. Eliezer Berkovits, *With God in Hell: Judaism in the Ghettos and Deathcamps* (New York and London: Sanhedrin Press, 1979), p. 111.

4. Berkovits, *With God in Hell*, p. 112.

Bibliography

General works

Argyle, Michael. *The Psychology of Happiness*. New York: Methuen, 1987.

Aristotle, *Nicomachean Ethics*. trans. Martin Oswald. New York: Macmillan Publishing Company, 1962.

Barrow, Robin. *Happiness*. Oxford: Martin Robertson, 1980.

Berger, Fred R. *Happiness, Justice, and Freedom*. Berkeley: University of California Press, 1984.

de Bono, Edward. *The Happiness Purpose*. Harmondsworth: Penguin Books, 1979.

de Botton, Alain. *The Consolations of Philosophy*. London: Hamish Hamilton, 2000.

—. *Status Anxiety*. London: Hamish Hamilton, 2004.

Brooks, David. *Bobos in Paradise: The New Upper Class and How They Got There*. New York: Simon & Schuster, 2000.

Dougherty, Jude P. *The Good Life and its Pursuit*. New York: Paragon House, 1984.

Edwards, Rem B. *Pleasures and Pains: A Theory of Qualitative Hedonism*. Ithaca: Cornell University Press, 1979.

Elbin, Paul Nowell. *The Paradox of Happiness*. New York: Hawthorn Books, 1975.

Eysenck, Michael W. *Happiness: Facts and Myths*. Hove: Erlbaum, 1990.

Frank, Robert. *Luxury Fever: Why Money Fails to Satisfy in an Era of Excess*. New York: The Free Press, 1999.

Freedman, J. *Happy People: What Happiness Is, Who Has It and Why*. New York: Harcourt, Brace, 1979.

Götz, Ignacio L. *Conceptions of Happiness*. Lanham, MD: The University Press of America, 1995.

Grayling, A.C. *What is Good?: The Search for the Best Way to Live*. London: Weidenfeld & Nicholson, 2003.

Griffin, James. *Well-Being: Its Meaning, Measurement and Moral Importance*. Oxford: Oxford University Press, 1986.

Jackson, Adam J. *The Secrets of Abundant Happiness*. London: Thorsons, 1995.

Kenny, Anthony. *Aristotle on the Perfect Life*. Oxford: Oxford University Press, 1992.

—. 'Happiness', *Proceedings of the Aristotelian Society* 66 (1965/6) 93-102.

Keynes, J.M. 'Economic Possibilities for Our Grandchildren', *The Collected Writings of John Maynard Keynes*. Vol. 9: 321-332. London: The Macmillan Press Ltd, 1972.

Kingwell, Mark. *In Pursuit of Happiness: Better Living from Plato to Prozac*. New York: Crown Publishers, 1998.

Kurtz, Paul. *Exuberance: A Philosophy of Happiness*. Buffalo and New York: Prometheus Books, 1977.

Lasch, Christopher. *The Culture of Narcissism: American Life in an Age of Diminishing Expectations*. New York: Norton, 1978.

—. *The Revolt of the Elites and the Betrayal of Democracy*. New York and London: W.W. Norton & Co., 1995.

Lloyd Thomas, D.A. 'Happiness', *Philosophical Quarterly* 18 (71) (April 1968) 97-113.

Marar, Ziyad. *The Happiness Paradox*. London: Reaktion Books, 2003.

McFall, Lynne. *Happiness*. New York: Peter Lang, 1979.

McGill, Vivian. *The Idea of Happiness*. New York: Frederick A. Praeger, 1947.

McMahon, Darrin. *Happiness: A History*. New York: Grove Atlantic, 2006.

Montague, Roger. 'Happiness', *Proceedings of the Aristotelian Society* 67 (1966/7): 87/102.

Morris, Desmond. *Happiness*. Birmingham: University of Birmingham Press, 1984.

Murray, Charles. *In Pursuit of Happiness and Good Government*. New York: Simon & Schuster, 1988.

Nozick, Robert. *The Examined Life: Philosophical Meditations*. New York: Simon & Schuster, 1989.

Nussbaum, Martha and Amartya Sen, eds. *The Quality of Life*. Oxford: Oxford University Press, 1992.

Pieper, Josef. *Happiness and Contemplation*. New York: Pantheon, 1958.

—. *In Defense of Philosophy*. San Francisco: Ignatius Press, 1992.

Powys, John Cowper. *The Art of Happiness*. New York: Simon & Schuster, 1935.

Putnam, Robert D. *Bowling Alone: The Collapse and Revival of American Community*. New York: Touchstone, 2000.

Rouner, Leroy S., ed. *In Pursuit of Happiness*. South Bend, IN: Notre Dame University Press, 1995.

Russell, Bertrand. *The Conquest of Happiness*. London: George Allen & Unwin Ltd, 1958.

Sachs, Hanns. 'Psychotherapy and the Pursuit of Happiness', *Imago* 1 (1939) 356/64.

Samuelson, Robert J. *The Good Life and its Discontents: The American Dream in the Age of Entitlement*. New York: Vintage, 1995.

Simpson, Robert W. 'Happiness', *American Philosophical Quarterly* (April 1975) 169/76.

Sumner, L. Wayne. 'Welfare, Happiness and Pleasure', *Utilitas* 4.2 (November 1992) 199/223.

Telfer, Elizabeth. *Happiness*. New York: St Martin's Press, 1980.

Tolstoy, Leo. *A Confession and Other Religious Writings*. Trans. Jane Kentish. Harmondsworth: Penguin Books, 1987.

White, Stephen A. *Sovereign Virtue: Aristotle on the Relation Between Happiness and Prosperity*. Stanford: Stanford University Press, 1992.

Wike, Victoria S. *Kant on Happiness in Ethics*. Albany, NY: SUNY Press. 1994.

The 'new science' of happiness

Robert Biswas-Diener, Ed Diener and Maya Tamir, 'The psychology of subjective well-being', *Daedalus* (Spring 2004), 18-25.

Csikszentmihalyi, Mihaly. *Flow: The Psychology of Optimal Experience*. New York: Harper and Row, 1990.

—. *Living Well: The Psychology of Everyday Life*. New York: Basic Books, 1997.

Diener, Ed and E. Suh. eds. *Culture and Subjective Well-being*. Cambridge, MA: MIT Press, 2000.

Easterlin, Richard A. 'The economics of happiness', *Daedalus* (Spring 2004) 26-33.

Easterlin, Richard, ed. *Happiness in Economics*. Cheltenham, UK: Edward Elgar, 2002.

Frey, Bruno S. and Alois Stutzer. *Happiness and Economics: How the Economy and Institutions Affect Well-Being*. Princeton, NJ: Princeton University Press, 2002.

Gilbert, Daniel. *Stumbling on Happiness*. London: Harper Press, 2006.

Haidt, Jonathan. *The Happiness Hypothesis: Putting Ancient Wisdom to the Test of Modern Science*. London: William Heinemann, 2006.

Kahneman, Daniel, Ed Diener and Norbert Schwarz, eds. *Well-Being: The Foundations of Hedonic Psychology*. New York: Russell Sage Foundation, 1999.

Lane, Robert E. *The Loss of Happiness in Market Democracies*. New Haven. CT: Yale University Press, 2001.

Layard, Richard. *Happiness: Lessons from a New Science*. London: Allen Lane, 2005.

Martin, Paul. *Making Happy People*. London: Fourth Estate, 2005.

Nettle, Daniel. *Happiness: The Science Behind Your Smile*. Oxford: Oxford University Press, 2005.

'Richer not happier: a 21st century search for the good life', *Royal Society for the Arts Journal* (July 2004), 36-45.

Seligman, Martin. *Authentic Happiness*. New York: The Free Press, 2002.

Tomkins, Richard. 'How to be happy'. *Financial Times*. 8-9 March 2003.

Veenhoven, Ruut. *Conditions of Happiness*. Dordrecht, Holland: D. Reidel Publishing Company, 1984.

Epicureanism

Annas, Julia. *The Morality of Happiness*. New York: Oxford University Press, 1993.

Cicero, Marcus Tullius. *On the Ends of Goods and Evils (De Finibus …)*. Trans. and ed. H. Rackham. London: William Heinemann, 1914.

—. *Tusculan Disputations*. Trans. and ed. A.E. Douglas. Warminster: Aris & Phillips, 1990.

DeWitt, Norman Wentworth. *Epicurus and his Philosophy*. Minneapolis: University of Minnesota Press, 1954.

Diogenes, Laertius. *Lives of the Philosophers*. Trans. R.D. Hicks. Cambridge, MA: Harvard University Press, 1958.

Epicurus, *Letters, Principal Doctrines* and *Vatican Sayings*, in *The Epicurus Reader: Selected Writings and Testiminia*. Trans. and ed. Brad Inwood and L.P. Gerson. Cambridge: Hackett Publishing Co., 1994.

Lucretius, *On the Nature of the Universe*. Trans. R.E. Latham.
    London: Penguin Books, 1951.
Hibler, Richard. *Happiness through Tranquility: The School of Epicurus*.
    Lanham, MD: University Press of America, 1984.
Rist, J.M. *Epicurus: An Introduction*. Cambridge: Cambridge
    University Press, 1972.
Strodach, George K., ed. *The Philosophy of Epicurus*. Evanston, IL:
    Northwestern University Press, 1963.

Utilitarianism

Barrow, Robin. *Utilitariansim*. Brookfield, VT: Edward Elgar
    Publishing Co., 1991.
Bentham, Jeremy, *An Introduction to the Principles of Morals and
    Legislation*, ed. J.H. Burns and H.L.A. Hart. 1791; Oxford:
    Oxford University Press, 1996.
Capaldi, Nicholas. *John Stuart Mill: A Biography*. Cambridge:
    Cambridge University Press, 2004.
Ebenstein, Alan O. *The Greatest Happiness Principle: An Examination
    of Utilitarianism*. New York and London: Garland Publishing,
    Inc., 1991.
Hobbes, Thomas. *Leviathan*, ed. Michael Oakeshott. New York:
    Macmillan Publishing Co., 1962.
Mill, J.S. *Autobiography of John Stuart Mill*. New York: Columbia
    University Press, 1924.
—. *Utilitarianism*, ed. Roger Crisp. 1861; Oxford: Oxford
    University Press, 1998.
Quinton, Anthony. *Utilitarian Ethics* 2nd ed. London: Duckworth,
    1989.
Ryan, Alan. *J.S. Mill*. London and Boston: Routledge & Kegan
    Paul, 1974.
—. *The Philosophy of John Stuart Mill*. London: Macmillan, 1970.

Hinduism

The Bhagavad-Gita. Trans. and ed. R.C. Zaehner. London: Oxford University Press, 1966.

Chaudhuri, Haridas. *Integral Yoga: The Concept of Harmonious and Creative Living*. London: George Allen & Unwin Ltd, 1965.

Flood, Gavin. *An Introduction to Hinduism*. Cambridge: Cambridge University Press, 1996.

Hamilton, Sue. *Indian Philosophy: A Very Short Introduction*. Oxford: Oxford University Press, 2001.

Klostermaier, Klaus K. *A Survey of Hinduism*. Albany, NY: State University of New York Press, 1994.

Kott, Kim. *Hinduism: A Very Short Introduction*. Oxford: Oxford University Press, 1998.

Organ, Troy Wilson. *The Hindu Quest for the Perfection of Man*. Athens, OH: Ohio University Press, 1970.

Mittal, Sushil and Gene Thursby, eds. *The Hindu World*. London: Routledge, 2004.

Pandit, M.P. *The Yoga of Knowledge*. Pomona, CA: Auromere, Inc., 1979.

Panigrahi, Sarat Chandra. *The Concept of Yoga in 'The Gita'*. Puri, Orissa: Prajnaloka, 1994.

Prem, Sri Krishna. *The Yoga of 'The Bhagavat Gita'*. London: John M. Watkins, 1951.

Radhakrishnan, Sarvepalli and Charles A. Moore, eds. *A Sourcebook in Indian Philosophy*. Princeton: Princeton University Press, 1957.

Satchidananda, Swami, ed. *Living Yoga: The Value of Yoga in Today's Life*. New York: Gordon and Breach Science Publishers, Inc., 1976.

Vivekananda, Swami. *Bhakti-Yoga: The Yoga of Love and Devotion*. Calcutta: Advaita Ashrama, 1974.

Zaehner, R.C. *Hindu & Muslim Mysticism*. Oxford: Oneworld Publications, 1960.

Buddhism

Armstrong, Karen. *Buddha*. 2000. London: Orion Books Ltd, 2002.

Carrithers, Michael. *Buddha: A Very Short Introduction*. 1983. Oxford: Oxford University Press, 2001.

Coleman, James William. *The New Buddhism: The Western Transformation of an Ancient Tradition*. Oxford: Oxford University Press, 2001.

Conradi, Peter J. *Going Buddhist*. London: Short Books, 2004.

Cope, Stephen. *Yoga and the Quest for the True Self*. New York: Bantam Books, 1999.

Dalai Lama, His Holiness. *Ancient Wisdom. Modern World: Ethics for a New Millennium*. London: Little, Brown and Co., 1999.

Dalai Lama, His Holiness and Howard C. Cutler. *The Art of Happiness: A Handbook for Living*. London: Hodder and Stoughton, 1998.

The Dhammapada. Trans. Juan Mascaró. Harmondsworth: Penguin, 1973.

Dumoulion, Heinrich and John C. Maraldo, eds. *Buddhism in the Modern World*. New York: Macmillan Publishing Co., Inc., 1976.

Humphreys, Christmas. *Exploring Buddhism*. London: George Allen & Unwin Ltd, 1974.

Keown, Damien. *Buddhism: A Very Short Introduction*. Oxford: Oxford University Press, 1996.

LaFleur, William R. *Buddhism*. Englewood Cliffs, New Jersey: Prentice-Hall, 1988.

Lopez, Donald S., Jr. *Buddhism*. London: The Penguin Press, 2001.

Mackenzie, Vicki, ed. *Why Buddhism?: Westerners in Search of Wisdom*. London: Thorsons, 2003.

Mitchell, Donald W. *Buddhism: Introducing the Buddhist Experience*. New York and Oxford: Oxford University Press, 2002.

Christianity

Aquinas, Thomas. *St. Thomas Aquinas on Politics and Ethics*. Ed. and trans. Paul E. Sigmund. New York: W.W. Norton & Co., 1988.

—. *Treatise on Happiness*. Ed. and trans. John A. Oesterle. Notre Dame, IN: University of Notre Dame Press, 1983.

—. *Virtue: Way to Happiness*. Trans. Richard J. Regan. Scranton, PA: University of Scranton Press, 1999.

Armstrong, Karen. *A History of God*. 1993. London: Vintage, 1999.

Chesterton, G.K. *St. Thomas Aquinas*. New York: Sheed & Ward, Inc., 1933.

Cupitt, Don. *Mysticism after Modernity*. Oxford: Blackwell Publishers Ltd, 1998.

Pieper, Josef. *The Silence of St. Thomas*. South Bend, IN: St. Augustine's Press, 1999.

Weisheipl, J. *Friar Thomas D'Aquino. His Life, Thought, and Works*. Washington, DC: Catholic University of America Press, 1983.

Islam

Al-Ghazali, Abu Hamid. *The Alchemy of Happiness*. Ed. and trans. Claud Field and Elton L. Daniel. London: M.E. Sharpe, Inc., 1991.

Armstrong, Karen. *A History of God*. 1993. London: Vintage, 1999.

Attar, Fariduddin. *The Conference of the Birds*, trans. C.S. Nott. London: Routledge & Kegan Paul, 1978.

Baldock, John. *The Essence of Sufism*. Royston: Eagle Editions, 2004.

Cragg, Kenneth, ed. *The Wisdom of the Sufis*. New York: New Directions, 1976.

Fakhry, Majid. *A History of Islamic Philosophy*. London: Longman,
    1983.

Macdonald, Duncan B. 'The Life of al-Ghazali', *Journal of the
    American Oriental Society* 20 (1899) 71-132.

Nasr, Seyyed Hossein. *Living Sufism*. London: Mandala Books,
    1980.

Quasem, Muhammad Abul. *The Ethics of Al-Ghazali: a composite
    ethics in Islam*. Selangor, Malaysia: Peninsular Malaysia, 1975.

—. 'Al Ghazali's Conception of Happiness', *Arabica* 22 (1975)
    153-61.

Shabistari, *The Secret Rose Garden*. Trans. Florence Lederer. Grand
    Rapids, MI: Phanes Press, 1987.

Shah, Idries. *The Sufis*. London: The Octagon Press, 1964.

Sharif, M.M., ed. *A History of Muslim Philosophy*. 2 vols. Delhi:
    Low Price Publications, 1961.

Sheikh, M. Saeed. *Studies in Muslim Philosophy*. Lahore: Ashraf
    Press, 1962.

Sheirf, Mohamed Ahmed. *Ghazali's Theory of Virtue*. Albany: State
    University of New York Press, 1975.

Smith, Margaret. *Al-Ghazali the Mystic*. London: Luzac & Co.,
    1944.

Umaruddin, M. *The Ethical Philosophy of Al-Ghazzali*. Aligarh,
    India: The Aligarh Muslim University Press, 1962.

Watt, W. Montgomery. *The Faith and Practice of Al-Ghazali*.
    London: George Allen & Unwin Ltd, 1953. (The text
    includes a translation of Ghazali's *The Deliverance from Evil*.)

—. *Muslim Intellectual: A Study of Al-Ghazali*. Edinburgh:
    Edinburgh University Press, 1963.

Zaehner, R.C. *Hindu & Muslim Mysticism*. Oxford: Oneworld
    Publications, 1960.

Stoicism

Aurelius, Marcus. *The 'Meditations' of Marcus Aurelius Antoninus* … .
Ed. R.B. Rutherford and trans. A.S.L. Farquaharson and R.B.
Rutherford. Oxford: Oxford University Press, 1989.

Boethius. *The Consolation of Philosophy*. Trans. Richard Green. New
York: Macmillan Publishing Company, 1962.

Cicero, Marcus Tullius. *On the Ends of Goods and Evils* (De
Finibus …). Trans. and ed. H. Rackham. London: William
Heinemann, 1914.

—. *Stoic Paradoxes*. Trans. and ed. M.R. Wright. Warminster: Aris
& Phillips, 1991.

—. *Tusculan Disputations*. Trans. and ed. A.E. Douglas.
Warminster: Aris & Phillips, 1990.

Colish, Marcia L. *The Stoic Tradition from Antiquity to the Early
Middle Ages*. Leiden: E.J. Brill, 1985.

Edelstein, Ludwig. *The Meaning of Stoicism*. Cambridge, MA:
Harvard University Press, 1966.

Epictetus. *The Enchiridion*. Trans. Thomas W. Higginson. New
York: Macmillan Publishing Company, 1948.

Long, A.A. *Stoic Studies*. Cambridge: Cambridge University
Press, 1996.

Long, A.A., ed. *Hellenistic Philosophy*. Berkeley, Los Angeles and
London: University of California Press, 1986.

Seneca. *De Vita Beata. Seneca: Four Dialogues*. Ed. C.D.N. Costa.
Warminster: Aris & Phillips, 1994.

Sorabji, Richard. *Emotion and Peace of Mind: From Stoic Agitation to
Christian Temptation*. Oxford: Oxford University Press, 2000.

Sørensen, Villy. *Seneca: The Humanist at the Court of Nero*.
Edinburgh: Canongate, 1984.

Stockdale, James B. 'Testing Epictetus' Doctrine in a Laboratory of
Human Behaviour', *Bulletin of the Institute of Classical Studies* 40
(1995) 1-13.

—. *A Vietnam Experience: Ten Years of Reflection*. Hoover Institution: Stanford, California, 1984.

Strange, Steven K. and Jack Zupko, eds. *Stoicism: Traditions and Transformations*. Cambridge: Cambridge University Press, 2004.

Tacitus. *The Annals of Imperial Rome*. Trans. and ed. Michael Grant. 1956; London: Penguin Books, 1989.

Wenley, R.M. *Stoicism and its Influence*. New York: Cooper Square Publishers, Inc., 1963.

Judaism

Andersen, Francis I. *Job: An Introduction and Commentary*. Leicester: Inter-Varsity Press, 1976.

Berkovits, Eliezer. *Faith after the Holocaust*. New York: Ktav Publishing House, Inc., 1973.

—. *God, Man and History: A Jewish Interpretation*. New York: Jonathan David, 1959.

—. *With God in Hell*. New York and London: Sanhedrin Press, 1979.

Frank, Daniel H. and Oliver Leaman, eds. *History of Jewish Philosophy*. London and New York: Routledge, 1997.

Frankl, Viktor E. *Man's Search for Meaning*. 1959. London: Random House, 2004.

Habel, Norman C. *The Book of Job: A Commentary*. London: SCM Press Ltd, 1985.

Kushner, Harold S. *When Bad Things Happen to Good People*. 1981; London: Pan Macmillan, 2002.

Perdue, L.G. and W.C. Gilpin, eds. *The Voice from the Whirlwind: Interpreting the Book of Job*. Abingdon, 1991.

Samuelson, Norbert M. *An Introduction to Modern Jewish Philosophy*. Albany, NY: State University of New York Press, 1989.

Acknowledgements

When I told my friends that I was going to write a book on happiness, I was expecting them to be supportive. After all, friends are supposed to support each other. Plus, everybody's interested in being happy, right? I was not, however, expecting them to tell me how to write the book. Yet in varying degrees, that is exactly what they did. Although I have not followed to the letter all of their instructions, I have been humbled by their generosity. With gratitude and affection I acknowledge the advice and support of John Brodholt, Cynthia Burns, James Davies, Ellen Gainor, Tom Hammack, Jim Holman, Steve Holman, Russell Hitchings, Sonja Kuftinec, George Marcotte, Joe Lordi, Ari Lipman, Stephen Orgel, Bill Patterson, Jeff Renzulli, Brian and Zanita Smedley-Aston, Adam Trexler, Michael Waring, and Aleksandra Wolska. Alan Stewart, a superb scholar who has also written for a wide readership, provided sound practical advice. Tony Morris, despite being an editor at another publishing house, was endlessly encouraging and offered insightful comments on portions of the manuscript. Andrew Leek listened patiently over many months as I recounted each advance – and each setback – in the long march from proposal to publication. Matt Richardson, a terrific writer, offered much needed help at a critical juncture. From the beginning, Richard Cellini's advice has been indispensable. No one could ask for a more astute reader, or a better friend.

Queen Mary, University of London, where I teach in the School of English and Drama, has been unusually supportive of this work. I thank Philip Ogden and Morag Shiach for granting me research leave to complete this book, and for encouraging me to write for a wider audience.

To my friend and agent Peter Robinson, sufficient thanks can hardly be given here, or anywhere. It is scarcely adequate to say that this book could not have been written without his patient guidance, innumerable kindnesses, and anchored confidence. Andrew Franklin at Profile Books never flagged in his enthusiasm for this project or in his support for an author new to the world of commercial publishing. Daniel Crewe has been the sharpest of editors and the book is all the better for his close and insightful reading of it. I am grateful to everyone else at Profile Books, especially Ruth Killick and Penny Daniel, for seeing this work through the production process with such devoted attention and Claire Peligry copy-edited the text with thoughfulness and care. I consider myself extremely fortunate – happy, even – to be published by Profile Books.

To this book's dedicatee belongs more honour than a mere dedication can bestow.

Index

Faust, 99–100

felicific calculus, 28, 31–3, 36–7
   see also Utilitarianism

flow, 18

fortune, 170–172, 178

Four Noble Truths, 97–104
   see also Buddhism

Frankl, Viktor, 199, 200, 201

freedom, 55, 193, 195, 197, 198–9

G

Gandhi, Mahatma, 84–5

Ganesha, 86–7

al-Ghazali, Abu Hamid, 10–12, 14, 21, 124, 133, 136, 140–44, 157, 206
   life as model for Sufi path, 148–9
   reconciles Sufism and orthodox Islam, 148–9
   see also Islam and Sufism

'greatest happiness', principle of, 28–30, 38, 39

goal, happiness as a, 17, 128–30, 131

gods:
   existence of, 53–4
   punishment by, 54–5

government's role in happiness, 34–6
   see also Utilitarianism

grace, 135–6, 138

H

hadith, 140, 145, 148, 149

Hamlet, 173

happiness:
   and action, 82–4, 89–90, 102–3, 129
   as activity, 18, 205
   in the afterlife, 117–18, 134–5, 138
   as alchemy, 12, 157
   approaches to:
      diversity of, 20–21
      unity of, 21
   beginnings of, 19–20, 155, 156
   cannot be achieved in isolation, 207
   and chance, 169–70, 170–171
   Christian conception of, 117–18, 124
   consumer market for, 2–3
   and contemplation, 124, 127, 130, 133
   and daily life, 81, 85–6, 92, 139
   and delusions, overcoming of, 94–5
   and desire:
      in Buddhism, 96, 97, 99–102
      in Christianity, 132
      in Epicureanism, 55, 56–7, 61–2, 63